HEALING
Neen

One Woman's Path to Salvation
from Trauma and Addiction

TONIER CAIN

Health Communications, Inc.
Deerfield Beach, Florida

www.hcibooks.com

Author's Note: This book depicts my life's journey and struggles from my perspective. Some of the events may not be pretty, but it is my story and my experience as seen and felt through the eyes and heart of a child, and then an addict, and now a woman in recovery. If I can help just one "Neen," then my struggles will not have been in vain.

Scriptures used throughout the book are taken from the New Living Translation unless otherwise noted.

**Library of Congress Cataloging-in-Publication Data
is available through the Library of Congress**

© 2014 Tonier Cain

ISBN-13: 9780757317965
ISBN-10: 0757317960
e-Pub: 9780757317972
e-Pub: 0757317979

Publisher: Health Communications, Inc.
  3201 S.W. 15th Street
  Deerfield Beach, FL 33442–8190

Cover image © Think Photography
Cover design by Dane Wesolko
Interior design and formatting by Lawna Patterson Oldfield

I dedicate this book to God,
whose Son thought it not robbery to leave
His glory and die that I might live,
to all who believed in me when I
didn't believe in myself, to those who will
be helped by my story, and to all the people
who love me and whom I love!

Contents

Preface

"For I know the plans I have for you,"
says the Lord. "They are plans for good
and not for disaster, to give you
a future and a hope.

—Jeremiah 29:11

I know most parents think their children are the best in the world. I'm not ashamed to say my youngest daughter, Orlandra, is the absolute best. She's smart. She's pretty. She's outgoing. When I look at her, I still marvel that God would give me another chance by giving her to me. Although I'd failed so badly at motherhood, He actually entrusted this precious little girl into my keeping. Sometimes when she's not looking, I look at her, and I can see the mercy and grace of God in her face.

I take her to school, and I am humbled by God's graciousness, because He has allowed me to send her to one of the best private schools. When I travel I take her with me, and I am speechless as I watch her holding intelligent conversations with lawyers and doctors, who are impressed by her inquisitive nature and her personality. Sometimes I look around and say, "Is this real? Am I the same Tonier Deneen Johnson Cain? This is not me." Sometimes I actually pinch myself to see if I am going to wake up and discover this is a dream because I haven't forgotten that, ten years ago, I was living on the streets of Annapolis.

Now I travel around the country training college-educated professionals about how to help people. I've met former presidents, corporate leaders, senators, and governors. I'm a homeowner with bills to pay. I'm living the American dream. But this dream didn't come without many nightmares; rather, it came as a result of tremendous cost and great sacrifice.

♦ ♦ ♦

On January 31, 2013, when Orlandra was in second grade, I took her to school as I always do. But this particular morning, I was having separation anxiety because I was waiting but not waiting. Orlandra looked up at me as I held her hand, and she said in her best big-girl voice, "Okay, Mommie. I can go by myself. I'm a big girl." She was right—she was getting so big and so independent. I looked down at her, and all the love I've ever had came pouring out. Tears came to my eyes, but I knew not to cry. Instead, I gave a little nervous laugh.

"I know," I said. "I just like holding your hand." And I started swinging her hand back and forth in a little game we play. She gave me that wonderful smile, and my heart melted. When I looked at her, I was once again reminded of the awesomeness of the Lord.

Just as we got to the classroom door, she dropped my hand and ran to her seat. "Orlandra!" I called. She turned around and ran back to where I stood just outside the door and gave me a quick hug. Then she quickly ran back to her seat. I still stood there frozen. Even though Orlandra is my sixth child, this motherhood thing was still new to me. Eventually, she looked back and saw me still standing there, and she shrugged her shoulders as if to signal me to leave.

She was right. It was time for me to leave. I had things to do before I went to work. But this morning I couldn't tame the uneasiness in my stomach. Orlandra was my anchor to reality. I was waiting, but I didn't want to appear to be waiting. Despite everything I'd lived through, I could still be disappointed, and I didn't want to be disappointed.

I remember thinking, *If I could just stop my mind from racing*. As I looked at Orlandra sitting at her desk talking to the little girl beside her, I wanted to cry. I felt the tears, so I blinked real hard. I got as far as the parking lot before the floodgates opened. I'd never done much crying when I lived on the streets, but now I cried if the wind blew in the wrong direction.

I left the school parking lot and headed to the gym. For the eight years I'd been sober, my sanctuaries have been God and exercise. I sweat and pray and recite my favorite Bible verses. That morning, I was pounding away on the treadmill, repeating in my head, *Delight yourself in the Lord and he will give you the desires of your heart . . . Delight yourself in the Lord and he will give you the desires of your heart* (Psalm 37:4, NIV). I kicked the speed up to 5, so I could get a brisk jog. I kept praying this scripture while listening to Marvin Winans singing, "Let the Church Say Amen."

After finishing my workout, I was still too wired up, so I called my cousin, who is also my stylist, and asked if she had an appointment available. To my great delight, she said, "Come on over!" Getting my hair washed would be a great distraction to take my mind off what I didn't want to acknowledge. When I arrived, the shop was filled with its usual group of stylists and clients talking the usual kind of women's talk—other people's business. This morning, my cousin, another stylist, and one of the clients were discussing Olivia and Fitz from the TV series *Scandal.* As I sat down in her chair, she asked the other stylist, "Girl, did you see last week's show?"

"You know I did. My kids and my old man know not to bother me when I'm watching *Scandal,*" she replied, as she applied perm solution to her client's hair.

"Did you see Fitz and Olivia? That white man can't get enough of that black woman. It was hot the other night! Oh Lawd!"

"Tell the truth! Uh!" They were laughing and having a good time, but my mind was elsewhere.

"Tonier, you don't watch *Scandal?*"

"Oh, no," I said. "If I'm not traveling, that's Orlandra's bedtime, and I'm trying to get her down. Don't have time to watch other people living in sin." We all laughed.

My cousin defended me by saying, "Tonier's always on the go. Let's go to the dryer." As I sat under the dryer, I put in my earbuds and cued up "Be Still" by Yolanda Adams. I closed my eyes and listened to the words of the song, as they spoke to my heart. I must've nodded off, but suddenly the music stopped and my phone rang. I put my glasses on and looked down. My heart skipped a couple of beats because I recognized the number. It was the Maryland Department of Social Services. I pressed the green button and said, "Hello?"

The voice at the other end said, "Good morning. Is this Tonier Cain?"

"This is she."

"Mrs. Cain, this is Cindy Root from the Department of Social Services. How are you this morning?"

"I'm fine," I said as I got up from the dryer and moved outside, so I could hear and talk freely.

"Well, I have good news. He said yes to a reunion." I held the phone away from my face and mouthed, "Thank you, Lord. Thank You! Thank You! Thank You!" At that moment, I knew God had answered my prayers, and the Holy Spirit in me said, "Delight thyself in Me, and I will give you the desires of your heart." Once again God had shown Himself mighty on my behalf. Somehow I managed to say thank you and get down the particulars. I wanted to shout but instead I wrapped my arms around myself and said aloud, "God, You are good all the time. And all the time, You are good. Thank You!" Then I went back into the salon to finish letting my hair dry.

The thing I'd been trying to avoid thinking about all morning was now a reality. For months I'd been working with the Department of Social Services to arrange a reunion with my youngest son, Joshua. It had been a long and involved process. But it was worth every phone call, every inquiry, every conversation, every prayer. Joshua had agreed to meet me.

◆ ◆ ◆

My journey to this day had been a long one. It started in a prison in 1994 when I laid before God and asked Him to help me. I'm sure my experience wasn't much different from a lot of other desperate people who come to God in times of need, but, in that cell, praying to a benevolent God, was a drug addict and prostitute who had been living on the streets of Annapolis, Maryland, for nineteen years. I'd been severely abused as a child and experienced severe trauma, and, as a result, I'd developed self-destructive behaviors.

When someone said I should write a book about my life, I smiled. I hadn't considered doing that, but, as I prayed about it, the Lord encouraged me to put my story in writing because it might help someone else and set them on the path to healing. So I write this book as the old song says, to "help somebody as I pass along; so my living is not in vain."

Introduction

"**M**iss Cain. Kin I speak to you?"

"Sure. Tell me what's happening with you." I walk over to a young woman dressed in gray prison garb. I am at the Maryland Institute for Women, where I'd been an inmate. I'm here now as a featured speaker to discuss trauma-informed care. As I approach her, she begins to cry.

"I lost my five children to the system. And I need help. Kin I attend your session?" Just the mention of a mother losing her children touches my heart. I know that pain. So I ask the warden if this woman can be a part of the small group session tomorrow evening, and she agrees.

I hug the woman and promise, "If you allow me, I'll help you. I won't leave you." I know the feeling of helplessness when the system designed to help fails. I know the despair when no one steps up to help you. It's one thing to be down, but it's another when you see no possibility of getting up, when being down becomes a way of life. I knew both. I'd been there.

The next evening in a small group session, this inmate tells me of a life of abuse that includes drug use and all that goes with it. As she cries and pours out her heart to me and the other women seated in a circle, I hear my story, or at least a form of my story. And I think, *But for the grace of God, I could still be here or dead.* I connect this inmate to a program that will allow her to get the assistance she needs to regain control of her life. The program includes trauma therapy, which will help her identify and acknowledge the things that had been done to her that contributed to her behavior.

This is my life now. I travel the country telling policy makers Neen's story. Neen is a form of my middle name that my family called me. It represents a past that almost destroyed my future; however, because of the intervention I received through trauma therapy, I emerged from that life and from the cycle the women I now speak to live in. Now I am committed to helping others break free from the shackles of secrecy that surround the abuse often caused by traumatic events.

Neen's story is not pretty. It shines the light of truth on the shady side of life in America. Much of it takes place in the dirty places of a beautiful city. It's about the smelly people you turn your head away from on the street corners and the ones you never think could be you or the ones you love. While the sad reality of Neen's story is that it continues to be repeated across this nation, there is hope for a happy ending. Because I broke the cycle and emerged stronger, I am able to offer a message of healing for others. No matter where you are on your journey, the message is: "Where there is breath, there is hope."

CHAPTER 1

Rough Beginnings

Beware that you don't look down
on any of these little ones. For I tell you
that in heaven their angels are always in
the presence of my heavenly Father.

—Matthew 18:10

"Life happens" is more than a bumper sticker; it's a reality that I know all too well. Life happened to me, although I didn't realize it at the time. From a very early age, people did things to me. I don't know if they singled me out or if I was just in the wrong place at the wrong time. I do know that, almost from the beginning of life as I knew it, things were done to me. As I grew older, I began to realize that the things that were being done to me were bad, but I was powerless to stop them or to get away from them. So "life" continued to happen, and I kept living as best I knew. Life was not always easy.

I'm not asking for sympathy; I'm simply telling the truth. I didn't have a good childhood, my teenage years were a drunken blur, married life was a disaster, my relationship with my mom was whacked, and the list goes on. I'd failed at so many things. I'd even failed at motherhood. But in the midst of all these happenings, I never gave up, because I believed that, as long as I had breath, there would always be a chance that my life could change.

There were times and places in my life when I thought my life would end, and, given the way I was living, it should've ended. I've been beaten and raped, almost had my head smashed in, used dirty needles, and smoked enough crack cocaine to heat a small third world country, but Someone kept me, and something kept me going. I didn't grow up in a churchgoing family, but I believed that, even in my lowest moments, there would be a better tomorrow. It was what kept me going in the midst of having things happen to me that were so horrific that, to this day, I am ashamed to speak of them; not because of who I am, but because of what other people did to an innocent child who couldn't defend herself. What happened to me was a "low-down, dirty shame."

I was born and grew up in Annapolis, Maryland, home to the U.S. Naval Academy and the capital city of the state of Maryland. It's a beautiful city, but Annapolis is a city of opposites: rich and poor. On one side of town are the wealthy people with yachts and big homes. On the other side of town are the projects. Strangely enough, one exists without seemingly knowing the other exists. When I was growing up in the projects, it was all I knew. For me it is the place of my birth and the beginning of my life of pleasure and pain.

There are many things from my childhood that I just don't remember. When I first became aware, I was about four years old. I was Tonier, and I lived with my mother, Barbara, and my father, Oatmeal, whose real name is Vernon Johnson. I had a sister named Bridget, and two brothers named Vernon Jr. and Carlos. We lived together in a two-story apartment in the projects.

Since I didn't know any other life, I accepted what I saw and heard in my mother and father's house. Sometime early in my childhood, I learned the sounds of living. No one taught me. No one said, "This is how you should live," or "This is how you shouldn't live." I became accustomed to how my parents treated each other and how they treated us. To me, "normal" was a life where people had fights and cussed at each other. I accepted what was because it was all I knew.

Oatmeal and Barbara fought a lot. It was one of the sounds I learned to recognize early on. Oatmeal would slap Barbara and push her down, and she'd scream at him. The sound of screaming, cussing, and hitting scared me and made me feel like there were butterflies in my stomach. I'd start to shake, the feeling would move into my chest, and my heart would start to beat really fast. Then the sound of fighting would move into my head. It wasn't a loud sound, but it made my heart beat even faster, and it filled my ears. Years later when I listened to a conch shell, it reminded me of that sound. Sometimes the sound took my breath away.

I remember screaming, "Stop! Barbara! Oatmeal!" But Barbara couldn't hear me above her own voice or Oatmeal's sounds. I'd be crying; everyone would be crying. But the crying didn't stop the beating, so I learned to hide from the sound. I learned to crawl into a ball and hold my ears. It didn't help. I could still hear, and so I cried and hid because Oatmeal was hitting Barbara. I learned when the talking became the sound that started the fight. It's strange what little children quickly learn.

"I ain't scared of you, Oatmeal! You can't make me do nothing. I still don't know why I married your sorry ass." That was Barbara's voice. Oatmeal said something back. Then Barbara said, "You can go now. Here! Take your shit and get out. Here, I'll help you. Take your ring. Naw. I tell you what, I'll put it where you can go—in the toilet."

"Go get it!" Oatmeal's sound was so loud.

"Get it your damn self. You want it." Then Oatmeal dragged Barbara down the hall to the bathroom. He had her by the back of the head, pulling her by her hair.

"You gone get it out of that toilet, or I'll flush you down behind it. Now get it." I guess Barbara couldn't get the ring because Oatmeal tried to put Barbara's head down the toilet. She was screaming; he was screaming. But this time even my screaming didn't make him stop.

There were a lot of scenes like this when I lived with Barbara and Oatmeal. Usually, they made up, followed by a lot of hugging and kissing. Then life went back the way it used to be until she made him mad again, and the sound would lead to another fight. I remember once we were at my grandmother Mil's house and Oatmeal punched his hand through a glass trying to hit Barbara. Years later when I learned about abuse, I knew that I'd grown up watching my father abuse my mother.

Once the sound of them fighting made me so sick, I couldn't breathe. They stopped fighting, and Barbara took me to the window and held my head outside so I could breathe. It was hot, and I couldn't stop throwing up. Nothing Barbara did made me better, so she took me to a doctor, who said I had asthma. When I woke up, I was in a big white tent. Looking for a window to breathe out of, like I did at home, I couldn't find one through the plastic. Scared, I yelled, "Barbara!" No one answered. "Barbara!" I was really scared because I couldn't remember where I was or how I'd gotten there. There were other beds in the room, but I didn't know who was in them. I kept calling for Barbara to come and get me. I wanted her to take me home. With all my four-year-old being, I wanted Barbara.

I never called Barbara "Mama" or "Mommie" or "Mudear," like the other children called their mamas. She was always Barbara. I don't know why, but my brothers, sister, and I always called her by her first name. I know now that names are important, but I was never taught to call her "Mama" or call Oatmeal "Daddy" or "Dad." All I knew then was that I was in a strange place, and I wanted Barbara.

"Barbara! Please come get me!!" But no one came to answer my call. I couldn't understand why Barbara would leave me. Didn't she love me anymore? "I love you, Barbara. I love you. I'm scared. Please come get me." After a while, I learned that no one would come when I cried, but it didn't stop me from crying. *Why were they doing this to me? Why?*

I don't remember how long I was in the tent or who finally answered my call of distress. As one day blended into another, I got accustomed to being there. I got used to the strange people around me. Then one day I woke up and Barbara was there.

"Neen. Neen! Wake up." I was so glad to see her.

"I wanna go home, Barbara," I pleaded.

"I know, Neen, but you gotta get better first." Barbara laid her hand on my head to see if I had a fever. Then she held my hand until I went to sleep. Once when I woke up, both Barbara and Oatmeal were there. On another day, I called for Barbara, but instead Sharon, my mother's sister, was there. I loved her and felt safe when she was there.

"Do you need to go to the bathroom? Come on, I'll take you." She took my hand and walked me down the hall to the bathroom. I remember thinking it was a strange bathroom. It wasn't like the bathroom at Barbara's house. I'd never seen a bathroom like this before. It was a large room with a lot of little rooms. I remember walking on the cold floor, and everything was white. Sharon took me to one of the little rooms and opened the door. Inside was a toilet with a hard black seat. She pulled down my panties and gently sat me on that hard, cold seat. I was scared that I was going to fall in, but I didn't say anything. I just held on to that hard black toilet seat and tried to do my business. As I sat there with my skinny legs dangling over the edge, I was so glad Sharon had come to see me. And I felt at peace.

When I finished using the bathroom, Sharon took me back to the big room where I slept in the tent. There were other children sleeping in beds like mine. I didn't realize it was the public hospital where poor people went. I still couldn't understand why I was there. Then I remembered my brother Carlos, who had died. In my four-year-old mind, I couldn't understand why if I were so sick, no one came to see if I was feeling better. No one ever came to hold my head out of the window like Barbara did when I couldn't breathe, and I missed and longed for Barbara, because at least she knew how to take care of me. I remember thinking, *I hope I don't die like Carlos* because, when you die, the police come and put you in a black bag. Then I wouldn't see Barbara, Oatmeal, Sharon, Mil, or any of my family anymore. I was scared that I'd die in that white tent.

I didn't really understand what happened when people died. I knew my sister Carla had died of an infection before I was born. I knew Carlos, my younger brother, had died of pneumonia. One day before I came to sleep in this tent, I remember hearing Barbara screaming, but she and Oatmeal weren't fighting. And she wasn't hollering at me or my sister or brothers. I remember sneaking up to the door of Barbara and Oatmeal's bedroom and looking in. She was standing by the little bed that Carlos slept in. Her sister Carol was there. It was one of the few times that I saw any of Barbara's family actually touching her. Carol had her arm around Barbara's waist.

"Oh God. I did the best I could. Oh! Carol, that's my baby. Look at him." It was Barbara, and she was talking to Carol, pleading for Carol to understand. And Carol did.

"He's in a better place now, Barbara. Don't nobody blame you," Carol said.

"I took him to that clinic. I did everything they told me. Ask Oatmeal. He was just too weak. Oh God! Help me!" Barbara was crying. She had her arms across her body like she was holding something. "Carol, you know I done my best!" Barbara cried.

"Barbara, you got to get ahold of yourself. You got other children to take care of. God don't make no mistakes. He took Carlos back to be with Him. The Lord gives, and the Lord takes away."

Barbara and Carol were standing over the bed, and Carlos was just lying there. I looked in and saw dried blood under his nose. He wasn't moving or crying or coughing. Barbara told Carol, "Don't pick him up. Leave him alone! Don't touch him, Carol." She just kept crying and crying. Eventually, Barbara went downstairs and told Oatmeal that Carlos was dead. I don't remember him screaming or crying. He just got up and left. Then, after a while, the police came, and some people picked up Carlos and took him away. He never came back. I thought that might be why Barbara was crying. She knew Carlos wouldn't be coming back. Then I heard that sound that made my stomach feel funny—it was in my chest and my ears. I saw Barbara crying. So I cried, too. It was one of the few times I remember seeing Barbara cry about anything while she was sober.

So now here I was in the hospital sick, and I was scared because I was alone. But when Sharon came, I felt better. She'd sit and hold my hand until I fell asleep. Then when I'd wake up, she'd be gone. But I never saw her leave.

There wasn't much to like about being in the hospital. I couldn't play with my sister, Bridget, or my brother, Vernon. The one thing I liked about my stay in the tent was these little packets of grape jelly. I remember someone opening those packets and squeezing it on my toast. I loved grape jelly. It was purple and sweet. After all these years, I still love grape jelly.

When I got better, Barbara sent me to her mother Mil's house, so Mil could take care of me. I loved my grandmother, but going home with Mil made me think that Barbara really didn't want me. *Why was Barbara sending me away again?* I loved Barbara. I wanted to go home with her so bad. I remember thinking if I could get better, she'd want me. *Please, Barbara. I won't get sick anymore. I won't get the asthma anymore. I promise. Please take me home. You can hold my head out the window if I can't breathe. Please don't leave me. Barbara! I need you. I love you!*

I didn't say anything because no one ever heard me, and a part of me wanted to go with my grandmother because, after Barbara, she was the one person in the whole world that I truly loved. She was also the only person who made me feel really safe. So I went to live with my grandmother, so she could take care of me until I got better. I was happy to be going home with her, but in my heart I longed for Barbara. And deep down inside I wanted to know why she didn't want me. That question plagued me for a long time.

My grandmother's name was Mildred, but we all called her Mil. I always felt happy when I was with her, and she kept me safe. At her house, I was the baby, which meant everyone had to be especially nice to me. When I'd wet the bed and my aunt Sharon would complain, Mil would say, "Leave that baby alone. And you'd better not hit her. She just a baby." I was actually five years old at this point, but I was still the youngest.

I thought my grandmother was the most beautiful woman in the whole world. She was the color of strong coffee, and her skin was so smooth. She wasn't skinny, but she wasn't fat either. In my eyes, she was exactly right. And, oh my goodness, did she smell good. I loved to sit in her lap and look at her skin. She'd smile and hug me. I knew she loved me. I could feel it. When I lived with Mil, I forgot the sound of Barbara and Oatmeal fighting. I learned the peace and safety of my grandmother's house.

At night, Rowe, who was Mil's husband, bought butter pecan ice cream for me and Neapolitan for Mil. I'd lie on the foot of her bed, and Rowe would sit beside the bed in a recliner. He'd take his bottle of Pepsi and pour peanuts into it. We'd eat our ice cream, and he'd drink his Pepsi as we all watched *The*

Carol Burnett Show. And Carol Burnett would sing, "I'm so glad we had this time together, just to have a laugh or sing a song. Seems we just get started and before you know it, comes the time we have to say 'so long.'" Mil would smile and say to me, "You my girl." And I knew I was safe and protected.

Mil's house was a good place in my five-year-old life. I had my cousin Deitra to play with and my aunt Sharon to worship and my uncle Butchey who made all of us laugh. While I missed Barbara, being at Mil's house was almost like being with my mother. The difference was that I had a clean bed and lots of good food to eat. I even had a friend named Tia who lived in a townhouse at the end of the row in Eastport Terrace Projects. Tia and I played together. She was the only friend I can remember from my childhood.

One day, Tia and I were playing in the street pushing a cart someone had taken from the local grocery store. Mil came to the door and called for me to come home. "Neen! Neen!" I heard her the first time, but we were having a good time, and I wasn't ready to go in. She came back to the door and called me, "Tonier Deneen Johnson." Now, everyone in our neighborhood knew if your mama called both your names, she meant business. I knew better than to ignore that call, but I stomped my foot because I was having too good a time to leave. Unfortunately, Mil saw me. I didn't know my grandmother could move so fast. Before I knew it, she had come down the apartment steps and grabbed me by the arm. She pulled me back up the street to the apartment.

"Did you stump your foot at me? No, ma'am. I *know* you didn't stump your foot at me. I'm going to give you something to stump your foot about, missy. Come on in this house."

"I'm sorry, Mil. I won't do it again." I was beside myself. I was crying and pleading at the same time.

"Oh, I know you won't do that again. You got the devil in you, and I'm going to beat him out. Stump your foot at me? I don't think so. Next you'll be talking back, and I don't tolerate no talking back in this house. Ask your mama what I did to her. Too grown-up to live in my house, the door can hit you where the good Lord split you."

I'd never seen my grandmother so angry with me. She really did beat the devil out of me. She held me by my arm and beat my backside and legs with a switch she'd pulled from a bush that grew beside the front door. I tried to grab her, but she'd push me away from her and continue to administer that switch around my legs. I thought it would last forever, but she finally stopped. Then she made me sit down on the sofa.

I'd had whippings before but not like this. Mil had beaten me. I couldn't stop crying. Mil had beaten me. Mil didn't let anyone beat me. After a while she called from the kitchen and said, "Stop that whimpering or I'll give you something to whimper about. I ain't gonna tolerate no hardheaded child. Not in my house. I'm shame of you. Neighbors seen you stumping your feet at me like you some grown woman." I sat there on the sofa sniffling. Eventually, I went to sleep because there is nothing like a good whipping to put a body to sleep.

When I woke up, Mil was sitting beside me on the sofa. "Come here." And she pulled me into her lap. "Do you know why Mil beat you?" I nodded my head yes. "I beat you 'cause I love you, and you have got to learn to mind. When I tell you to do something, you got to do it. I wouldn't never do anything to cause you harm. Do you understand?" I nodded my head yes.

"Mil?"

"Yeah."

"I'm sorry. I love you. I won't be bad no more." I wrapped my arms around my grandmother's neck, and I held on for dear life. At that moment, I would've jumped off the tallest building in the world for my grandmother. I just wanted her to know I loved her so much, and I was truly sorry for the way I'd acted.

"I know you love me, baby, and I love you. Now don't cry no more. Guess what Mil cooked for you while you were sleep?" I could already smell the wonderful aroma coming from the kitchen.

"Pork chops!" I screamed in delight.

"That's right," Mil said as she stood up with me, my arms still wrapped around her neck and my legs wrapped around her body. "Pork chops 'n' mashed potatoes 'n' collard greens 'n' cornbread. Just for you!" I remember squealing for joy. Then

Mil called the rest of the family, "Butchey, Carol, Deitra, Rowe. Y'all come on and eat. Dinner is ready."

My grandmother was the best. One Saturday, she took me downtown to a department store in Annapolis. I was so excited. I'd never been to a store downtown, and it was a big deal that we rode the bus. There was so much that I'd never seen before. We got on some steps that moved. I held on to Mil's hand because, although I was scared, I was with my protector. She held my hand and smiled down at me. I thought I'd died and gone straight to heaven. There were so many people.

There were racks of beautiful clothes. I'd never seen such a sight in my life. I could barely breathe. This was a truly wonderful place. I was so excited that I forgot to tell Mil I needed to go to the bathroom. I was afraid if I stopped to go to the bathroom, this magical place would vanish. So I didn't tell her. By the time I started holding myself and dancing, it was too late, and I wet myself. I was a bed wetter, but I'd never wet myself during the day. I was so ashamed, but Mil didn't get upset or beat me. She just finished her purchases and took me home. I went to sleep on the bus ride back. I guess shame also made me sleep.

One of the happiest days of life at my grandmother's house was the first day of kindergarten. Mil had bought me this beautiful all-white jean outfit. The night before she'd washed my stubborn hair and straightened it in the kitchen. Getting my hair "did" was always a major event. Mil sat me on a stool beside the stove in the kitchen. She'd part off a section of my hair and apply some Old 97 Hair Grease. Then she'd take the metal straightening comb that had been heating on the stove and pull it through my hair. The problem was the sizzling sound the grease made, and the heat on my scalp made me flinch and dodge. That made Mil pull even more and made me dodge even more. It always ended with her burning me and me screaming. It was a painful experience for both of us. Eventually, however, she'd succeed in pulling all the natural curl or "nap" out of my hair, and it would lay straight and long down my back.

I thought I was so pretty. My hair was long and straight. Mil just beamed when she looked at me. I don't think I slept at all that night. I do remember that I didn't wet the bed that night. The next morning Tia and I walked hand in hand to the bus stop. I was so happy. Life was truly good.

My grandmother didn't work, so she was always home when I came home from school. Most days she'd be in the house cooking and watching her "shows." But sometimes her friend Miss Louise would be at the house. Some days when I came home from school, Mil and Miss Louise would be sitting on the stoop drinking Coca-Colas. They'd be talking, and I could smell cooked food coming from our house.

Miss Louise would always ask me the same thing: "Neen, did you learn all the teaching in school?" I'd grin and shake my head. Then Mil would say, "Don't shake your head, baby. Answer Louise."

"No, ma'am." Then I'd turn to my grandmother and ask in the same breath, "Mil, can I go play with Tia? Pleeze?"

"Go take off your school clothes, and you can go. But play on the sidewalk, so I can see you. And what I told you when you go to other people's house?"

"Don't eat nothing even if they offer." I remembered that because Mil reminded me every time I went to Tia's house. I was never sure why I couldn't eat there, but I knew I couldn't, and I didn't!

I liked living at my grandmother's house, although I did miss Barbara and my sister and brother. Sometimes Mil would try to get me to go spend the weekends with Barbara, but I was so comfortable. And as much as I missed Barbara, I'd settled into the routine at Mil's. Life was so good that I didn't realize changes in my grandmother. She still cooked; Rowe still bought us ice cream. I still played with Tia. Butchey made wonderful bracelets out of forks. Deitra and I still shared Sharon's room. But something was happening to my grandmother, something no one explained to me or Deitra.

One day Barbara showed up and said she'd come to take me home. I was about nine years old. I cried because I didn't want to leave my grandmother, and I didn't want to leave my best friend, Tia. I loved my life. Mil made me feel safe. Aunt Dorothy also came and took Deitra home. They just said that Mil was not well. She didn't look sick, but I'd learn within the year just how sick she really was.

I remember asking her, "Mil, do you have the pneumonia?"

"Naw, baby. Mil just got a little something-something going on right now. I'll be okay. I'm in God's hands."

"Why I can't stay with you? I'll make you better," I pleaded.

I didn't know it then but my life was about to change in ways that I couldn't imagine. I also didn't know that I'd only see my grandmother alive a few more times, and she'd be so changed. The last time I saw Mil, we'd all gathered at my aunt Dorothy's house for a cookout. All Barbara's sisters and brothers were there—Charles, who we called Jumbo, Carol, Butchey, and Sharon.

What struck my heart was my grandmother. She was so changed. It had been maybe a year since I'd moved from her house. When I left, she stood at the door and waved at me. Now she was sitting in a wheelchair, too weak to walk. No one had told me she was sick. No one had prepared me for what I saw. I wanted to help her, but I didn't know how. She didn't cook those wonderful smothered pork chops I loved so well. I remember thinking she looked so tired.

Mil, I love you. I'll take care of you. I can come back and live with you, and me and Rowe will take care of you. Mil, what can I do? Does it hurt? I'll be good. I promise. Just get better. That is what my heart said, but my mouth said nothing. I just stood beside her chair all day and held on to the arm of that chair trying to connect to the only person with whom I had always felt safe and loved.

Going back to Barbara's house was so different. All the things I'd taken for granted and become accustomed to at Mil's house were gone. I'd lost my school friend, Tia; I'd lost the clean, safe haven I had with my grandmother. All the good food was gone. By the time I went back, Oatmeal was gone, too. I never knew where or why, but he wasn't there. In addition to Bridget and Vernon Jr., I now had another little brother named Terance and a baby sister named Teli. It was just us and Barbara. And I learned new sounds, like the sound of being hungry because Barbara would sell the food stamps. I learned to be afraid because Barbara would leave for days. She'd lock us in her hot apartment and go wherever grown people went. What was surprising is we never went out looking for her, and no one reported we were left alone.

We knew better than to leave the apartment. Because I was the oldest, I learned to be the provider. One time she left us, we were so hungry. So I tried to open a can of the government meat with a knife, the way Barbara did. I put the pointed part of the knife on the can and hit the handle with my other hand the way I'd seen Barbara do. Something went wrong and my hand slipped. I was cut and bleeding. Blood was everywhere. I started to scream. The other kids started to scream. I was scared I'd bleed to death. For once I broke the rule, unlocked the door, and went to look for Barbara. Sure enough, I found her at the apartment where she'd hang out. When she came to the door, she was eating a fried chicken sandwich. Although

I was in pain and bleeding, I remember looking at her eating while she'd left us hungry and locked in her apartment. At that moment, I realized Barbara really didn't care whether we ate or not, and, if we ate, it would be our responsibility.

I remember another time we were so hungry I asked Barbara if she could call Mil to come fix us some pork chops. "I ain't got to call no damn body. I kin cook." So she went into the kitchen and opened a can of green beans. Then she mixed in some mayonnaise. It smelled bad; it was nasty. So I refused to eat it. That made her mad. I heard the sound that usually meant I was about to get a real beat-down.

"You too good to eat what I cooked? Huh? You too damn good? Well, you kin go hungry." With every word, she started poking me in the side with a butcher knife. I'd been beaten before, but I was really scared Barbara would kill me. If I died, who would look out for my brothers and sister? Mil wouldn't know until it was too late. There was nobody to care about them. I kept hearing this sound in my head, even as I screamed and fell off the chair. I thought she'd stabbed me, but she'd just been poking me with the handle of the knife.

Life with Barbara was hard. I loved her so much, but she seemed to be in her own world. Most of the time she just ignored us, but if we managed to get on her nerves, which we often did, it would mean the worst kind of beating. She'd hold the end of the belt and beat me. I quickly learned to answer when she called.

"Neen! Neen! You hear me calling you."

I heard her. I didn't want to hear her. So I buried my head under the covers. *Oh man, somebody peed last night.* Now the sheets were not only stinking, they smelled like old and new pee, and I was wet. *Oh, please let me go back to sleep and wake up at Mil's house. Please let me go back to sleep. Please.* I squeezed my eyes shut, pulled the covers back up, and went back to sleep. I think.

I had to be asleep. I was having the most wonderful dream. I was not in Newtown Twenty Housing Projects. I was back at my grandmother's house. I was sleeping in the room I shared with Sharon and my cousin Deitra. But none of them were in my dream. It was just me and my grandmother.

"Come on, baby, get up. I done cooked you something special this morning." It was my grandmother's voice. She pulled back the covers, and I was clean and I didn't stink from pee. "Come on, Tonier, get up. Deitra! Get up. The morning is flying by. Get up and go wash your face." Mil picked me up in her arms and carried me down the hallway to the bathroom. I was dry. Sometimes I'd wet the bed, but not last night. My T-shirt and panties were both dry. She washed my face and smoothed my hair.

"Lawd, girl, I don't know where you got all this hair from." She laughed as she smoothed down my stubborn,

nappy hair. "After breakfast, I'm gonna put some more grease on it and replait it. That oughta help."

Then we were at the table where Mil had set out fried sausage, scrambled eggs, and toast with butter on both sides. She spread some wonderful grape jelly on the toast and gave me a slice, which I started to tear into.

"Just a minute. We got to thank the Lawd for this meal." In Mil's house, you never ate a meal without saying grace, and you never went to bed without saying your prayers.

"Okay. Bow your head. Can you say the grace?" I nodded my head. "Okay. Let's say it together." So I bowed my head and put my hands together like Mil had taught me.

"God is great and God is good. And we thank Him for this food. Amen!" I was so proud because I remembered the whole grace. And my grandmother was pleased.

"You gone be a Christian yet. Now eat your food."

And eat I did. I always ate all my food. I was always hungry, and Mil always cooked the best food in the whole world. My favorite meal was her smothered pork chops. She'd fry those pork chops and sauté onions and bell peppers, then she'd make a gravy and put those pork chops back in the gravy. Oh, Lord! Then she'd cook these buttery mashed potatoes. It was oh so good. One thing God had given my grandmother was the ability to cook!

When breakfast was through, she combed my hair.
That was always an ordeal because I had a head full of
"stubborn, nappy Negro" hair. That is how my grand-
mother described it. And I was tender-headed, which
made a bad situation even worse. But Mil was gentle.
"I know, baby. Mil gone take her time. But I got to
untangle this mess. Do you want to look like Angela
Davis? Great big ol' Afro." I didn't know who Angela
Davis was or what an Afro was, but it made Mil laugh,
so I laughed, too.
Then she rubbed some Old 97 Bergamot on my hair,
parted it in the middle, and combed it out so she could make
little bushy ponytails. I ducked as best I could, but she held
me between her legs and worked on my head. In about twenty
minutes, I looked like the other little girls in the neighbor-
hood. I had four big bushy ponytails. Mil said I looked
"beautiful." And I believed her. She hugged me. She smelled
like sausage and coffee. I loved Mil.

"Neen! Dammit! I know you hear me. Um gone to beat the
natural black off you!" I was awake now. I was hot, and I was
back in Barbara's apartment in Newtown Twenty Apartments.
It was always so hot because Barbara's apartment didn't have
air-conditioning. So the heat was stifling. Added to the heat
was the smell of living: body odors, stale beer, urine, and sweat.

I jumped up just as the door to the bedroom I shared with my brothers and sisters opened. There was Barbara. At one time I think my mother was probably an attractive woman, but now she looked tired, probably from the drinking and from last night and all the children she'd had but didn't take care of. I still thought she was beautiful.

"Neen! Git up and git these chirren ready. You going to school this morning."

I didn't say anything. I seldom said anything in reply to a demand from Barbara. I didn't want to run the risk of "pissing her off" because I knew that meant a real beat-down. So I just jumped up and started shaking my brothers and sisters. As I ruffled through the mounds of clothes on the bed and the floor to find something, Barbara called one last time.

"Come on, let's go. The bus gone be here in a minute." I rushed them into their clothes. I couldn't tell if they were clean or not. It didn't matter; Barbara was letting us go to school. It was a good day! I loved school. Then she opened the door and walked into the mess that was the bedroom I shared with my siblings.

"I smell shit. Did you change the baby?" As I turned to gather up the baby and change her diaper, I didn't see Barbara's hand. She hit me in the back. *Thud!*

"You ain't going nowhere. Your head so damn hard. If you'd got your behind up when I called the first time, you woulda had time to change that baby. Well, since you didn't, just stay home and do it. I know damn well you ain't crying, 'cause I'll give you something to cry about." She grabbed me by the back of my head and spun me around. I wasn't crying. I knew better. I also knew better than to say anything. So I dropped my head and turned back around to take the dirty diaper off the baby.

"Git that mess off that baby." With that command, she slammed the door and left. I was so disappointed. I really liked going to school. It wasn't that I was a good student. It was just time away from Barbara and all the pain that living with her brought. School was my escape, although it was a different kind of nightmare. I went dirty and smelly, which made me the object of the other children's scorn. They called me names and picked on me constantly.

"Pissy Neen! Pissy Neen! Face is dirty and your drawers ain't clean."

"Raccoon girl! Raccoon girl! Look lak a great big squirrel."

They made up rhymes to mock and belittle me. It worked. I never fought back or said a word. I'd just stand there and look at them. The girls ignored me or made fun of me while the boys said cruel things about me. I know it sounds strange, but while going to school was painful, I preferred being there rather than at Barbara's.

My schoolmates were mean in the way only children can be mean. Not one of them ever tried to be my friend. They never passed me notes. No one ever asked why I came to school dirty and smelly. No one ever asked me about my mom. Nobody ever picked me to be on a team or participate in a ring-play. Instead, they'd point and stick out their tongues at me. So most of the time, I spent my recess time hiding in the restroom. But as bad as it was at school, it was so much better than being locked up in Barbara's nasty, hot apartment. I remember one day the teacher found me hiding and crying in the girl's restroom.

"Tonier? Tonier?" I looked up and there stood Mrs. Moore, my teacher.

"Ma'am?"

"You know you shouldn't be in the restroom without permission. Let's go. Get back out to the playground." I needed her to ask me what was wrong. I needed her to ask why I came to school so irregularly. I needed her to ask why I came to school smelling of urine. I needed her to care. I needed. But she just stood there and pointed at the door. Inside I was screaming, *Mrs. Moore! Please help me. Mrs. Moore, please ask me what is wrong! Mrs. Moore, can't you hear me? Mrs. Moore?* But I didn't say anything. I just stood up and shuffled out of the restroom. She didn't hear me. She didn't care if I existed.

◆ ◆ ◆

Tomorrow I'd be quicker. Tomorrow I'd get up before Barbara and get the children ready. Tomorrow when she said we could go to school, we'd all be ready. Tomorrow. But the reality of today said the children were hungry. So I waited a few minutes until I heard the outside door slam. That meant Barbara was gone, and I was free to hunt for whatever scraps of food that were left from last night's party.

Barbara, I need you. I need to tell you what that man did to me last night. He hurt me. He hurt me bad. Don't you care? Barbara! Barbara! We're hungry. Please don't leave. That's what my heart cried, but I just wandered into the dirty kitchen to find food for us because my sisters and brothers depended on me. I had to feed them. I had to protect them. If I was lucky, Barbara had left some food from last night. But first I found the cups of half-drank beer and wine and quickly drained them. Somewhere along the line, my nine-year-old mind had learned that the way to dull the pain was in the bottom of a cup. It took away the memory of last night, but it didn't dull the hunger in my stomach or the ache in my heart.

After scrapping around, I finally found enough leftover pieces of cold meat and added it to some of the government cheese, and we had breakfast. We didn't have eggs and toast with grape jelly like I used to have at Mil's house, but we had something to fill our stomachs. And we'd all learned to eat what was there because there were times when there wasn't anything. We hadn't been taught table manners or training, so we didn't know how to use forks or napkins. We just ate, and we were glad to be eating. I forgot the grace I'd learned at Mil's house, but later, when I remembered it, I made my sisters and brothers repeat it. I did it because I felt like my grandmother would be pleased. And I imagined she was watching over me, so I'd say the verse to please her.

Most of my days from the age of nine to eleven were spent inside Barbara's hot, dirty apartment. I never knew where she spent her days or what she was doing. I just knew that when she went out, we never let anyone into the apartment. By now Barbara had two other babies. I had a brother named Dante and another brother named Monterae. I didn't know about how people got pregnant or had babies, I just knew that, after a while, Barbara would bring home another baby. And life would go on as before.

One day we were all playing in the front room, and Barbara was there. I heard steps coming up the stairs. Usually the steps would stop, but these steps kept coming. Then someone knocked on Barbara's door. It was too early for Barbara's party. The men usually didn't come until night, and I could see the sun shining through the sheets at the windows.

"Yeah," Barbara said.

"Barbara, this me. Open the door." It was Dot. It was Barbara's older sister.

We all started screaming, "Dot! Dot!" We all ran to the door because she always bought us something, or she brought Mil over to cook us something to eat. When I opened the door, she was not smiling. She hugged us, but she didn't have anything to give us, and Mil was not with her.

"Barbara." Then she started to cry. "Barbara, Mil died." Suddenly my sense of smell came to life. I remember smelling the heat in the apartment, and I could smell the dirty dishes in the kitchen sink. But above all these scents, I smelled something else. It was new, and it was strong. I smelled my own helplessness. I didn't know it was that. I just knew I had this knot in my stomach. Up to that point in my life, I had always known that my grandmother would come to see about us. Now she was gone, and I somehow knew there was no one to save me. There was no safe place anymore. There was no one to come and protect me. I was helpless.

In that hot apartment, it felt like time had stopped. Then it all came apart like a bomb. Boom! Boom! Barbara was screaming and crying. Boom! Dot was crying. I was crying. Bridget, Vernon, Terance, Teli, Dante, and Monterae were all crying. I remember thinking, *Please stop.* I held up my hands. If I could just stop, but I couldn't stop anything, and my world was falling apart.

"Mil! Aw, God, no. No, God! Not Mil! Don't leave us. Naw! Naw! Dot, what we gone do without her? Aw naw. Naw! Naw!" It was Barbara's voice. Dot tried her best to calm Barbara down, but it didn't work. Barbara was wringing her hands and pulling at her clothes. I remember Dot had her hands folded like she was praying, and she looked so helpless. She looked so lost. What were we going to do without Mil?

At first Barbara fell on the floor, and then she got up. There was a plastic flower pot beside the sofa, and she threw it against the wall. It broke and pieces flew all over the room. That seemed to wake Dot up because I remember hearing her say, "Come on, Barbara. Mil wouldn't want you to act like this."

"Don't tell me how d'hell to act. Dis my mama! Dot, dis my mama!" After a while, I guess, Dot gave up. Because Barbara kept hollering and crying, so finally Dot came over and patted us. Then she just left. We were scared. We were crying. And it was hot. It seemed like Dot's news about Mil's death had made the room even hotter. With my grandmother's death, I now knew there was no one to care about us or look out for me. It was just us and Barbara, and, while I loved Barbara, I didn't trust her to protect me or provide for me.

CHAPTER 2

Stolen Joy

Let the children come to me.
Don't stop them!
For the Kingdom of God
belongs to those who are like
these children.

—Mark 10:14

I f Barbara failed at being a mother, she didn't fail at being a party girl. So while I didn't know names like Sly and the Family Stone, Aretha Franklin, or the Temptations, I knew their music because Barbara played it. I also knew her moods by the music she played. When she was getting ready for a party, she'd be singing. She'd be moving around the apartment, cleaning fish or chicken and dancing. Sometimes she'd dance with me or my brothers or sister. Barbara really was fun sometimes. And she was so beautiful when she smiled. She'd be excited about the party, and we'd be happy to just be with her.

"Come on, baby. Do the bump with Barbara." We'd try to keep up as she wiggled her hips and bumped into us as she took swigs from a can of Budweiser or a glass of something. But we weren't very good, and, after a while, she'd just dance alone. Barbara was a great dancer, and I loved to watch her. Then we'd hear a knock on the door.

"Hey, Barbara! BB. Bad Barbara, sexiest lady in the whole town. Sound lak you done started the party without me." It was one of the many nameless men who had come to party with Barbara. I didn't think it was strange then, but now I wonder why no women ever came. After a while, they'd be drinking and eating. Sometimes, she'd dance with them. The music would be thumping, and I knew it was time to herd my brothers and sisters into the hot bedroom we all shared.

At nine years old, I'd started to be the mother to my brothers and sisters. So when they looked at me and said, "Neen. We hongry," I knew I had to find some food somehow. One night, I snuck into the kitchen to steal a piece of fish. Barbara caught me and beat me back down the hall. "Take your silly behind back to bed." She smelled of fried fish and beer. It was strange that Barbara always had food for her partying friends, but we were always hungry.

I remember longing for my grandmother and her marvelous cooking. I would've given anything for some of Mil's smothered pork chops with collard greens and cornbread. "Barbara. We hungry! We ain't had no dinner. Can we have a piece of fish? Please?" That's what I wanted to say, but I knew better. I knew if I said too much to Barbara, she would've really beaten me, so I went back down the hall and closed the door. I knew there'd be a time when she and most of her company would pass out. Then I'd slip out and get us something.

One night when the music died down, I heard someone shuffling down the hall toward the bedroom where we all slept. I knew it wasn't Barbara, so I got up and stood at the door. The door opened, and there stood one of Barbara's men friends. I thought at first he was looking for the bathroom, but he grabbed me and pulled me into the hallway. I could see Barbara lying across the couch. She was sound asleep.

He pulled me into Barbara's bedroom and closed the door. Then he started to do things that I knew were wrong. He touched me. He put his mouth on mine and began sticking his tongue in my mouth. I tried to turn my head. He was breathing hard and fumbling with his clothes. I struggled to get away from him, but he held me down. Then I felt him as he began to touch my "pocketbook." I started to kick, but he was too strong. He did things to me that no child should know about. When I realized I couldn't get away from him, I stopped struggling. I didn't scream; who would hear? After that first time, I didn't cry; who would care? I just endured it. It was another sound I'd have to learn.

The sad thing about this part of my life was that it happened more times than I am able or want to remember. Yet Barbara didn't seem to notice, and I couldn't tell her. So I became hard inside, like if I didn't feel anything, it wouldn't hurt. After a while, it didn't hurt. I'd brush my teeth to get the taste of them out of my mouth, and I'd wash between my legs to wash off the feel of them. All this happened while Barbara was asleep in the next room.

Barbara, wake up! They are hurting me. Wake up and protect me. Wake up! But she didn't wake up, so she couldn't make them stop. So the hurting and the suffering continued. From that point on, I never felt safe in Barbara's house because I never knew when one of her "friends" would come after me. I couldn't tell anyone because no one cared. No one would believe me. So I kept quiet and brushed my teeth.

What was amazing was I still loved Barbara. In spite of the fact that she didn't protect me, I still loved her, and, more than anything in the world, I wanted her to love me, too. I knew what those men did to me was wrong, but if I told anyone I was afraid they'd take me away from Barbara. So I never told, not even Carol. I couldn't bring myself to admit that Barbara had failed me. If Mil were here, I know she would've protected me, but Mil was dead.

Then one day, we were alone in the apartment playing as we always did when Barbara was out. I heard footsteps coming. At first I thought they were going to another apartment, but they kept coming. And I knew it was not Barbara or even any of the "friends" who came to party. The steps I heard were different. I knew the sound of Barbara's footsteps. For some reason, I was scared. I didn't know why. I just knew something bad was about to happen. I knew it. Inside I heard that sound. My heart started to beat real fast, as the butterflies moved in my stomach. When the knock came, I went to the door and cracked it a little. There was a white man in a suit, a black lady, and a police officer.

The man spoke, "Is your momma home?" He was peeking over my head into the apartment. I shook my head. "I'm Mr. Livingston from the Department of Social Services, and this is

Mrs. Lewis and Officer Turner. Are you the oldest?" I shook my head again. "Are you Toner?" I laughed because he'd mispronounced my name.

"My name is Tonier," I said, looking from him to the lady who was busy writing something in a notebook. Then she turned to the officer and said something.

Finally the lady said, "Tonier, can we come in, honey?" It wasn't so much a question as it was a statement because with that she stepped in front of Mr. Livingston and pushed the door open. All three came into Barbara's house. Barbara don't want nobody in here when she ain't home. Barbara gone be mad if she come and y'all in here. Y'all gone be sorry when Barbara comes. That's what my heart said, but, as usual, I said nothing. I just went over and stood by the couch. They looked around at the apartment, which was in its usual condition: filthy. They walked into the kitchen where the sink was filled with unwashed dishes that had soured and started to grow black mold. They opened the refrigerator, which was empty except for some cheese, a pot with some beans, and a jug of water. They looked in the bedrooms with all the clothes on the floor. They could smell the urine and see the cigarette butts from last night and the beer cans in the garbage can. They saw it all, but they didn't see Barbara.

After a while, they walked out of the apartment and stood by the door talking. I remember thinking, *Something bad is going to happen*. The sound was roaring in my head. But I

I had to protect my sisters and brothers, until Barbara came. *Where was Barbara? Barbara, please come home!* My brothers and sisters were clinging to me. I'd become their protector, but I was scared myself. Finally, Mrs. Lewis came and sat on the edge of a chair. She had all of us sit down on the couch. Her voice sounded so nice, but the words that came out of her mouth tore our world apart.

"Tonier, I need for you to be a big girl. We have looked around at your mom's apartment, and it's not clean. There is no food in the refrigerator, and you and your sisters and brothers are unclean. We can't leave you in this house. Do you understand?" I just sat there looking at her. What was she saying? What did those words mean? "We can't leave you here," she said. "We are going to take you to a safe home." When she said that, I understood, and I jumped up screaming. For the first time since all the many things that had been done to me had started, I spoke up for myself and my brothers and sisters.

"You can't take us away! Barbara won't know where we at and she'll be mad. I want Barbara. I want Barbara." Now all the other kids started to scream and cry. We were so scared, and Barbara was nowhere to be found. But we knew she'd come back. She always came back.

Mrs. Lewis proved to be very nice. She sat and talked to us to calm us down. She kept telling me that we'd be back together. She even promised us they'd tell Barbara where we were. I didn't know if she was telling me the truth or not, but it made me feel better. I wasn't happy about going, but I felt better knowing that Barbara would find out where we were because I knew she'd come and get us.

Eventually, several other policemen and other social workers showed up. They split us up, except me and Bridget. I remember sitting with Bridget in the back of a car and watching another car pull off with Terance, Teli, Dante, Monterae, and Vernon. I remember Bridget and I hugging each other and crying again. I was never as scared as I was at that moment. I was trembling inside. All that I knew was being destroyed, and I couldn't stop it. I couldn't do anything but sit in the back of this car that was speeding away from the only home I knew. I was going somewhere, but I had no idea where. Thoughts kept running through my head: *Why are they doing this to me? What have I done wrong? I tried to keep the children when Barbara was gone. I tried to fix them food. I tried to protect them. I never told about the men and what they did to me. I never told. I hope Barbara won't be mad at me. I tried.*

I didn't know how long we traveled or in which direction, but we finally stopped in front of a house. It wasn't an apartment, either. It was a real house with a porch. The lady in the front seat turned and said to me, "We're here." I was really scared now. Barbara wouldn't be able to find this place. My stomach began to hurt, and I had to go to the bathroom real bad, but I didn't say anything.

A black lady opened the door. She seemed to have known we were coming. She shook hands with the social workers. Then she turned to me and introduced herself. I didn't want to know her. I wanted Barbara. I wanted to go home. Where were Terance, Vernon, Dante, Teli, and Monterae? Where were my sister and brothers? They'd be scared without me and Barbara. I wanted to go home. I couldn't understand why we couldn't go home. *Why were they doing this to me?*

I don't remember much about that foster home, except the kitchen table. I can remember sitting at that table and crying and crying. I wanted Barbara. I longed for my sister and brothers. I missed our home, and I wanted to go home. Barbara could take care of us. I wanted us to be together again as a family. I wanted Terance, Teli, Vernon, Dante and Monterae to be with me and Bridget. The foster parent did all the right things. She fed us. She gave us clean clothes. She was nice, but she was not Barbara. I was lonely, lost, and confused. And all I wanted was Barbara. We only stayed there for a few nights, but it seemed like forever.

One morning, the social workers showed up and took us to court. When we got there, I was the happiest I'd been in days because I was able to see my sisters and brothers. I thought, *It's going to be all right now.* Just as the social workers had told me, we were back together, and there was Barbara.

We were brought into what I later learned was a courtroom. Up front was a man in a black robe, and he was in charge. I,

along with my sisters and brothers, were seated up front on a
bench. Then I really looked around the room. I don't know why
I hadn't noticed before, but there were all Barbara's sisters and
brothers and our cousins. There was Oatmeal, whom I'd not
seen since I left to live with Mil. I kept thinking, *Why are they
all here?* I soon found out why.

The judge called for Barbara to come stand in front of him.
He was so mean. I wanted to scream at him to stop because
he was making Barbara cry and wail. I wanted to yell, "Stop,
you don't know anything about Barbara. I love her. She is my
mama! I want to go home with Barbara," but I said nothing.
I just sat there and listened as he told her she was not a good
mother, how she'd endangered the welfare of her children. All
this time Barbara was crying. Oatmeal just stood there looking
like he was frozen in time. Nobody said anything good about
Barbara. Nobody stood up for her. *Why didn't they say something good about her?* Not Sharon or Carol or Butchey; nobody
said anything to make that judge stop. He said:

Let's see. Case #34251. The State of Maryland versus
Barbara Johnson. Please step forward. I am going to go
off the usual record and talk directly to you, because I am
appalled by your actions. These are your children. Yet you,
Mrs. Johnson, have allowed these children to live in what
can only be described as a pigsty. I have looked at pictures
taken of the apartment where you left these children, and

it is despicable. I have presided over many cases, but I have never seen a case as bad as this. Why or how you have been allowed to continue to have custody of these children is a mystery to me, but it's a condition that I intend to remedy. I have in hand a report that details how you leave these children alone for days. I have statements from the social workers that detail the frequent parties that occur at your home.

Mr. Johnson? I understand you do not live in the home; however, you are as much to blame as your wife. Are the two of you still married? Why haven't you been more active in these children's lives? Have you even bothered to check to see how they were living? If I had my way, I'd put both of you in jail. Unfortunately, I don't have that ability. What I do have is the ability to safeguard the lives of these children, and I intend to do just that.

I have been informed there are family members present who have agreed to take these children to keep them out of the foster care system. I commend you. We need families who will keep the kids together. Yet I can't help but wonder where each of you has been, and why you have not intervened. We are going to correct this situation this morning.

I am ordering the immediate removal of these children, and authorizing the placement of them with the relatives who are present. Mrs. Johnson, you will not have contact with these children for one year. In that time, you are to

complete state-supervised parenting classes. You are to
report for monthly drug and alcohol testing. If after that
time, this court finds you are able and "fit" to have these
children, the court will reevaluate custody at that time.

Barbara stood there crying and shaking, and no one
defended her. Carol didn't tell how Barbara had taken care
of Carlos before he'd died. Sharon didn't tell about how Barbara would hold my head out the window when I had asthma
attacks. Nobody told how even though she went out, she always
came back. No one said anything good about Barbara, and I
couldn't understand why. Why weren't they speaking up for
her? If Mil had been here, they wouldn't be treating Barbara
like this. Mil would've defended Barbara! I knew it.

Sure, Barbara liked to party and have a good time, but she
did the best she could. Why was this man allowed to cause her
so much pain? Couldn't he see he was causing us pain? Didn't
he know that when he hurt Barbara, he hurt us? Why was he
doing this to me? Why were we made to sit there and hear all
those terrible things about Barbara? Did anyone think about
how it would make us feel?

When the judge announced that he was removing us from
her custody, I remember hearing Barbara scream. My head
turned to her, and, almost like it was orchestrated, we all began
to cry. Me, Bridget, Vernon, Terance, and Teli in that order.
But it didn't stop the judge, who began auctioning us off to

whoever would take us. When I came into the courtroom, I was glad to see my sisters and brothers. I had no idea it would be the last time we would be together as a family.

Terance was given to Oatmeal. Vernon went with our cousin Ann's sister, Janice. It was never talked about much, but everyone seemed to know that Dante was not a Johnson, so he went with his grandmother. Monterae went with Ann's brother, who we called Cousin Man, who eventually adopted him. Bridget went with Carol, and Teli went with Oatmeal's brother's ex-wife, Ella Mae. And that left me—alone and ashamed. No one wanted me. Finally, Ann stood up and said she'd take me.

If I couldn't live with Barbara or Mil, Ann was my next choice. I was glad she'd chosen me, although I was the last to be selected. Ann was my mother's cousin, although we sometimes called her aunt. She was married and had three daughters. To me they were perfect. They were always clean, and they were so smart. That day for the first time in a long time, I felt like my life was turning around. The awful smell of helplessness was gone. Even though I was sad, I actually left that courtroom feeling like I'd be all right. I felt as if something was coming back to my life. I didn't know what it was at the time, but after a few weeks at Ann's house, I realized it was hope.

Because Ann lived only a few blocks from the courthouse, we walked to her house. As we walked away from the courthouse, Ann talked to me. "Neen, I'm glad you are coming home with me. It's gone be all right. You and the girls will sleep together. You know them. It'll be just fine." Ann was trying to keep me calm as I continued to sniffle and look backward toward the big building where I'd left all semblance of the life I knew. "You'll be okay. God is watching over you, and I believe Mil would be glad you are going to be with us." That really made me feel better knowing that Ann remembered my grandmother and thought she'd be pleased.

Ealker, Stacy, and Ty, Ann's daughters, all welcomed me. I guess she'd already told them that I might be coming to live with them because they didn't seem surprised to see me. They treated me like a part of the family. Now, instead of being in charge of other children, I became the little sister. They looked out for me. They'd take turns combing and trying to tame my very nappy hair. It didn't hurt when they did it, and it was fun. For the first time since living with Mil, I was starting to enjoy a real childhood again. Being at Ann's house was so different from what I was used to. For one thing, the house was clean and it smelled nice. There were no clothes on the floor. She'd cook for us and feed us. There was a television set. Most important, there were no drunken men touching me. I felt safe and protected. It reminded me of Mil's house.

It was at Ann's house that I first learned what real family life should be. I shared a room with Ann's girls, which had a twin bed and a set of bunk beds. I slept on the bottom bunk with Ealker. It was so nice to sleep with one person instead of six. But the best thing about living with Ann was that I didn't have to care for or clean up behind anyone but myself. And Ann treated me like I was one of her girls.

It was Ann who taught me how a girl should take care of her body. Although I was almost a teenager, I'd never been taught the basics of personal hygiene. One morning, I woke up and there was blood in my panties. I was so afraid I'd done something wrong. I had flashbacks of those men getting up off me and the feel of something slimy that would be left between my legs. I was afraid they had put something in me that was coming out. What if they had given me a disease? I was so scared, so I shut up. And I shut down.

When Ann realized that I'd started my menstrual cycle, she came and sat down with me. She explained that what was happening to me was normal. She took me into the bathroom and showed me how to use the sanitary products. She was so kind and so patient. I was so ashamed because I thought I'd done something really wrong. I wanted so bad to tell Ann about what those men had done to me, but I didn't. I was just happy that I was not dying from some incurable disease they'd given me.

"You just turning into a little woman," she said. She then informed me that this would happen every month, and I should tell her when it happened. She even gave me a calendar to put up in the closet, so I could mark off the days when my period was on. I was so glad I was with Ann. She explained how I should wipe myself, and how to wash. She was not embarrassed, which made it easy for me. She told me personal things about caring for my body. Things Barbara should've told me.

I quickly fell in love with Ann and her family because they never blamed Barbara for the state I was in, and they accepted me. I think Ann may have known something had happened to me, but she never asked. And I never told. Finally, I was part of a real family. In addition to Ann and the girls, her father, Uncle Speed, also lived with us. Uncle Speed, who was a barber, always smelled of Ben Gay. He'd sit quietly in his bedroom, and every so often he'd call us in and give each of us a quarter.

Life at Ann's house quickly settled into a routine. Because she didn't want me to have to change schools, she arranged for me to get back and forth to my old school. And I actually started to enjoy going to school. I was clean, and the kids didn't pick on me anymore. My school work improved. I was finally fitting in. I was safe.

Every Sunday, we'd go to First Baptist Church. I don't know why, but I loved going to Sunday school. It may have been because, although they called it Sunday school, it wasn't like regular school, and I learned wonderful things about Jesus and God. I loved the stories from the Bible. I remember learning, "For God loved the world so much that he gave His one and only Son, so that everyone who believes in Him will not perish but have eternal life" (John 3:16). I also learned the Lord's Prayer. "Our Father, who art in heaven, hallowed be Thy name. Thy kingdom come, Thy will be done on earth as it is in heaven.

Give us this day our daily bread, and forgive us our debts as we forgive our debtors. And lead us not into temptation, but deliver us from evil, for Thine is the kingdom and the power and the glory forever. Amen." I didn't think much about how those verses and this prayer would play such a significant role in my life later. I just memorized them with the other children. Much later in my life when I was in life-and-death situations, these verses and that prayer would automatically come to me.

I sang in the children's choir, although I really couldn't sing, but everyone made me feel welcome. During the services, I'd sit mesmerized as the teachers talked about how God loved mankind, and Jesus loved the whole world.

When I was about twelve, I got baptized. I didn't truly understand the whole thing about salvation, but I wanted to please God. Mostly, I wanted Him to love me. I thought if God could love me, then I'd have someone who could protect me. And all they said I had to do was "believe" that Jesus could save me from my sins. So I prayed and asked Him to forgive me. Then I just believed with a childish faith.

My first Christmas at Ann's house was unbelievable. When I lived with Barbara, the only gifts we got were from the people at Angel Tree or the Salvation Army. So it was hard to imagine my delight when I got up that morning, and there were gifts with my name on them. I was so excited. This was too good to be true.

"Ealker, look what I got. Look what Santa Claus bought me! Ty. What you got? Lemme see!" For once, I think I truly didn't remember Barbara and all the hurt she'd brought upon me. I was just a child enjoying Christmas for the first time since I'd left my grandmother's house. It was wonderful. Ann had cooked. She wasn't as good as my Mil, but it didn't matter. I was happy, and all I heard was love.

After that first Christmas, time seemed to just fly by. My position in the family was settled. I'd stopped wetting the bed. Those sounds that I'd heard at Barbara's had gone away completely. I was doing well in school in part because Ann realized I was squinting when I did homework, so she arranged for me to get my first pair of glasses. I was safe and I was happy. Then one afternoon, I was upstairs doing my homework when I heard a familiar voice.

"Neen! Neen! Where my girl? I come to get my girl. I love you. Neen! Where you at?" I couldn't believe it. It was Barbara. After three years, she'd come back, and she wanted me to come home with her. I ran to the top of the stairs and stopped. I was so excited about seeing her. I truly loved my mother, and there she was, wanting me to come back to live with her. And she'd actually said out loud what I had always longed to hear: she loved me. With those three words, she'd wiped away all the things that had happened to me at her house, and, sadly, she'd wiped away all the goodness I'd found with Ann and her family.

"Barbara! Barbara!" I flew down the stairs and into her arms. We did a ring dance, where she was spinning me around and looking me over.

"Look at you. You done growed up. Getting so big. You 'bout to be a young lady." And I was so proud of myself because I had become all of those things. My hair was neatly combed. I was clean. I was well fed. I hadn't stopped to think much about it, but I guess I did look pretty good. Now here was the only person I loved above all others saying she loved me and wanted me back. It didn't take a minute for me to decide. I was going home with Barbara because she loved me.

I was so excited I could barely pack my belongings. As I packed all the nice things Ann and her family had bought me, they were crying like I had died. I couldn't understand it. They should've been glad that my real mother had finally gotten herself straight and wanted me back. She must've satisfied that judge and now she was "fit" to raise me. But Ann and her daughters kept crying. I saw something in Ann's eyes, but I didn't know what it was. Later I'd understand, but not that day. Barbara was here, and she wanted me to come home.

"Barbara, we gone get Terance, 'n' Bridget, 'n' em?" I asked as I hurriedly packed.

"Huh-uh. Hurry up now. We got to go." So I hurried to end an ideal phase of my life—a phase that I'd look back at and long for in the not-too-distant future.

CHAPTER 3

Harsh Reality

Then he said to me,
"Speak a prophetic message
to these bones and say,
'Dry bones, listen to the word
of the Lord!'"

—Ezekiel 37:4

I barely remember the ride back to Barbara's apartment because I was so excited to be going home with her. Most important, Barbara had said she loved me, and she wanted me back. I was so happy! Home had changed, though. Barbara had now moved to Meade Village, another public housing project. When I got back to her house, I was surprised to find that, in the three years I'd been living with Ann, Barbara had not only moved, she'd had three more children.

"Neen, remember your little sisters. Shannon, 'n' LaTonya, 'n' Tyra. Y'all know your big sister Neen." Barbara introduced me to the new babies. They didn't seem to care who I was. I thought they were cute, but I realized that, in the three years since I'd been gone, Barbara had been too busy having more babies to miss or care about me. That hurt because I never forgot her. That evening, even though we'd been apart for so long, she went out.

"Neen, I got to make a little run. I'll be right back." With that she was out the door and gone. There I was again with three new babies who were depending on me. All of my excitement about being back was gone. As the door slammed, I suddenly realized she didn't really want me back. She didn't love me. I was her convenience. I was fourteen years old, and it wasn't a week before I realized why Barbara needed me: I became the official babysitter.

If I acted indifferent or pretended not to know what to do for one of the little ones, Barbara would snap and say, "Neen, you big enough now to see 'bout these babies without me telling you everything. What's the matter with you? You act lak you don't know nothin." I wanted to scream, "I know plenty now. I know how to wash myself. I know about God. I know how to sing. I can read. I know how to feel safe. Ann taught me things you didn't teach me. Ann bought me Christmas gifts." But it hadn't taken me a week to relearn the sound of Barbara's anger. So I kept my mouth shut and kept the children as best I knew how. To speak up would've meant a beating, and I was getting too big for the beatings. So I kept quiet. But inside I was boiling. I didn't want to be in charge. I didn't want these children depending on me. Living with Ann and her girls had taught me that life had hope. But now I had lost my voice, as I realized there was no hope.

By the time I got back to Barbara's house, Oatmeal had returned Terance. And Teli was back. I never knew if Ella Mae had brought her back or Barbara had gone to get her. Either way, there we were—me, Terance, and Teli—back living with Barbara and our new sisters.

I missed going to school. I missed First Baptist Church and singing in the children's choir. I told my brother and sisters about how Ann put up beautiful decorations for Christmas. I impressed them by telling them how Uncle Speed would give us quarters. I told them about how nice Ann's house was. I bragged about my life with Ann because I truly missed it. And I hated that that life had ended. I was sad, but I was also experiencing something I'd never allowed myself to experience before: anger. I'd believed that I had a chance, but it was all a great big lie. So I shared stories with my little sisters and brother because they'd listen. But I knew I couldn't say anything to Barbara.

Before I went to live with Ann, the nasty apartment, wild parties, and filth didn't bother me because it was all I knew. Now, however, I'd seen how other people lived. I'd lived a better life, and it made being with Barbara that much more difficult. What I wanted was not a priority to Barbara. She hadn't changed. Her nights were spent partying with her friends. That meant someone had to take care of her children, and that person was me. I resented her for it. For the first time in my life, I became hostile about what was being done to me. But I was powerless to do anything about it. So I suffered in silence.

One morning, I decided that I was going to school regardless of what Barbara said or did. So I got up and got ready. I thought Barbara was asleep, but she'd already gone across the street to an apartment where she'd go to drink and hang out. I bolted out the door and down the steps to the bus stop. Barbara saw me and came running out of the apartment across the street. She caught me in the middle of the street and beat me like I'd stolen something.

"Neen. Where d'hell you think you going?"

"Please, Barbara. Please. I wanna go to school," I begged her.

"You wanna go to school? I'll teach you 'bout sneaking out the house without my permission. You gettin' too grown for your own good." She'd tackled me and was sitting on top of me. She began beating me with her fists. I threw up my arms to cover my face and that seemed to make her madder.

"You tryin' to hit me? You tryin' to hit me! I'll beat the very black off of your behind. You little heifer. Don't you never raise your hand at me. I brought you in this world, and I'll damn sho take your sorry behind out. Now get up and get your butt back up them stairs."

Then in front of the entire neighborhood, she made me go back to the apartment to care for my siblings. It wasn't the beating that hurt me that morning. I'd had plenty of beat-downs from Barbara. It was that no one stopped her. All the neighbors saw. I felt so ashamed. I couldn't say why. It was not like Barbara hadn't beaten me before, or that people even knew it. There was just something different about it this time. As I think back on that incident, I wonder why none of them called the police or Child Protective Services. But no one called, and no one came to see why the Johnson children were not in school. No one cared about me. That was the question in my heart and head: *Why doesn't anyone care about me?*

I had started to care about me, and I couldn't take living with Barbara anymore. She was right. I was growing up. So I decided I was going to run away, and I told Terance my plan. I'd never run away before, and I think Terance thought it was a big game. So he asked me, "Kin I run away wid you? Pleeze, Neen. I kin run fast. Take me wid you." I agreed on the condition that he wouldn't tell anybody. A few days later I whispered to Terance that, when I went to take the trash out, I was going to run away.

Next to the apartment complex was a wooded area where the police regularly found the dead bodies of dope addicts, but it became our escape route. When I went to the trash Dumpster, I threw in the garbage. Then I looked around. Nobody was looking, so I said to Terance, "Run." And we ran through those woods like the devil himself was behind us. My fear of Barbara catching us outweighed my fear of what could've been in those woods. I ran like a slave escaping to freedom. I remember looking over my shoulder every so often. I was so scared that somebody would appear from nowhere and grab us. "Run, Terance!" And we ran like the wind because I knew if Barbara caught us, she'd beat me to within an inch of my life. I didn't go back to Ann's because I knew that would be the first place Barbara would look. Instead, I took Terance to Ann's sister, Janice, who lived in Lake Village, a nearby community.

When we came out of the woods, both of us were out of breath. Neither of us could speak. We were tired, but I was more driven by my fear. So when we left the woods and were back on the street, we didn't stop running. In fact, I kept running and looking back over my shoulder. I kept expecting that at any minute Barbara would come out of a door, run me down, and beat me like she did the morning I tried to go to school. But no one appeared.

When we knocked on Janice's door, someone let us in. Janice lived in a two-story townhouse. I remember going directly upstairs to the bathroom. All I could think about was how hopeless my life had become. I didn't want to live. I wanted to die, because I thought I might see Mil. So I opened the medicine cabinet and grabbed as many pill bottles as I could and emptied them into my hand. Then I put every pill I'd found into my mouth and took a gulp of water from the sink. I just stood looking at my reflection in the mirror. Then I saw my grandmother.

"Mil! Mil!"

"Neen! Baby, what you done?" It was my grandmother. She was alive, and she was talking to me. It looked like we were in her kitchen in Eastport Terrace Projects. And Mil was cooking. I could smell that pork chop dinner. "What's the matter? You kin tell me. What's wrong?" I was sitting on that stool where she used to make me sit when she was doing my hair. She put her hands on my shoulders and looked at me. She was so beautiful. "Tell Mil."

So I told her all the things that had been done to me. About how Barbara would let me go hungry and beat me with the belt. I told her about the drunken men who forced themselves on me and all the pain they had caused me. I told her about how I was so afraid. About how Barbara had fooled me into leaving Ann's house and about all the things that I'd been too ashamed to tell anyone. I told her all the things that no one had bothered to ask me. I cried, but I told my grandmother because I knew she loved me. I knew she'd make things better. I told her because she was the first and only person to ever ask me what was wrong. She started to hug me, and then I heard a sound.

It was the sound of me gagging from what felt like a hose down my throat. "Tonier? Tonier? Open your eyes. Open your eyes!" As I slowly opened my eyes, I realized I was in a hospital, and some strange white man was peering into my face while a nurse held a basin. "Can you hear me?" I just looked at him. "What's your name?" At first I didn't respond. Where had Mil gone? "Mil? Mil?" I tried to say her name, but they had that hose down my throat. When they pulled it out, I was throwing up. Big globs of green stuff were coming out of my mouth.

"You are at North Arundel Hospital. Can you hear me?" Then the man said something to a nurse. I just laid there with tears running down my face because I realized that Mil was not there, and it was all a dream.

Then the doctor asked, "Are the parents here? I'll talk to them. She's going to be all right. Go ahead and get her cleaned up. I think we'll keep her a day to make sure she doesn't have any adverse effects from the medication." I never said a word to that doctor. I didn't make a sound, but I cried because I'd failed to kill myself, and I knew the pain would start again when I went home with Barbara. So I lay there in North Arundel Hospital, and I cried.

When I woke up again I was in a room. Barbara and Oatmeal were there. I didn't say anything because my feelings didn't matter. I didn't want to live. I wanted to die and go back to where Mil was. So I said nothing. Eventually, I learned that Barbara had told the doctors I'd accidentally taken too much of my medication. That was another lie. In retrospect, I can't believe that not one doctor or nurse thought I may have tried to commit suicide. But no one did, and not one counselor, therapist, or social worker came to talk to me. I knew then without a doubt that what happened to me didn't matter to anyone. I knew there was not one person who cared a damn thing about me. I knew that I was totally and completely on my own. Whether I lived or died, no one really cared. I knew this, and I was only fourteen years old!

After two days, I went home with Barbara. Since I had no hope, and nothing I did mattered to anyone, I started doing something I'd not done in three years: I started drinking. When Barbara was out of the apartment, I'd steal her beer or any other alcohol that was in the apartment. If she set a glass down, I'd drain what was left because the alcohol took away the pain.

Barbara noticed my changed attitude, and I think she was a little frightened by what I tried to do. She knew I wanted to die. I think she realized, at least in part, that I was genuinely unhappy. At this point, any rational human being would've tried to change to help her daughter. She should've known my attempted suicide was a cry for help, but she either didn't know or she didn't understand. Instead, she offered to send her problem to someone else.

"If you don't wanna be here, you kin go live with Carol." That was the solution to her Tonier problem. Did she dare ask *me* what was wrong? Did she ask me why a fourteen-year-old girl would rather die than live? *Don't you want to know why? Don't you care?* That's what I wanted to say, but instead I said nothing. I just packed my things and joined my sister Bridget at Carol's house.

Life at Carol's house was better in so many ways. For one thing, Carol's house was clean and food was plentiful. She'd married a wonderful man named Earl Johnson, but everyone called him Peter Rabbit. Carol and Rabbit were good to me, but by the time I joined them, I was so deeply wounded and had so much baggage that I could barely function. In addition to everything that had happened to me, I was also a functioning alcoholic. Although I was back in school, I couldn't begin my day without a beer or two.

Some days I'd wait until Carol and Rabbit left for work, and then I'd steal a beer out of his cooler. If I missed my beer at home, someone would have some alcohol at the bus stop. Other times, I'd purchase a quart bottle of grapefruit juice from the store on the corner. I'd pour out half of the grapefruit juice and fill the bottle with gin. Then I'd sip off it all day. No one seemed to realize what I was doing—until one day in gym class.

Usually, I was in control of myself, going about the school day without any teachers knowing I was drunk. But one day, Mrs. Palmer, our PE teacher, made us do gymnastics. "All right, Tonier, up on the balance beam," she instructed. I don't know whether it was because I jumped up too quickly or the height of being that far off the floor, but the minute I got up on that beam, the world swirled. I didn't just lose my balance; I fell, and I fell hard. Mrs. Palmer came running over to me, afraid I'd injured myself. I was amazed that she didn't smell the liquor on my breath, but she didn't. At least she acted as if she didn't.

"Johnson, are you awright?"

"I can't do this stupid beam." I'd learned that a good defense was to pretend to be offended. So I'd developed a real attitude. Not only did it keep people away from me, it protected me from the pain people always caused me. So I just got off the floor and strutted over to the wall to nurse my wounded pride and calm my shattered, drunken nerves.

By this time I was fifteen, and I begged Carol to let me get a job. At first, she was very much against the idea. "Neen, I have got to see you keeping your grades up."

"I can do it. It won't interfere with school. Pleeze," I begged.

"Where's this job, and what kind of hours are you talking about?" asked Carol.

"It's at Emporium Pizza Parlor. The manager is a black woman. It's part-time right now. She knows I'm in school, so I'd work four till closing two nights a week, and every other weekend I'd rotate shifts. Pleeze, Carol. I'd have some spending money. I'd even give Bridget some money. Pleeze!"

"Aw right. But if I see you are falling behind in school, that's the end." I was so excited. I was going to have a job, which meant that I'd have my own money. But rather than think of how I could use the money toward my future, my first thought was, *I can help Barbara.* But working at the Emporium soon provided me with more than just money. It became my source for my drug of choice: alcohol. At the end of every shift, I was allowed to drink pitchers of beer.

The manager at the pizza parlor and I had become good friends, and while working there, I met her brother, Keith Cain, who was also a friend of Barbara's. Keith was a good guy. He was fun to be with, made me laugh, and treated me like an adult. I liked him; he was the nicest man I'd ever met. Even though he was an older guy, he didn't attempt to take advantage of me in any way. We were just good friends. He'd hang around after we closed. Then he'd invite me over to his mother's house to continue drinking. One night after drinking at his house, Keith and I both passed out. When I woke up, it was 6:00 AM. I knew I was in trouble. Rabbit always left for work around 5:00 AM, and Carol would be up. I was panicked. Carol would have a hissy fit. "Keith! Keith! Wake up. You got to take me home now. Come on." I shook Keith to wake him. He grumbled, but he got up. That was the longest ride across town.

When we got to within a block of Carol's, Keith dropped me off at the corner. I let myself in and tiptoed to our bedroom. Bridget was still asleep, so I just fell on top of my bed. It felt like I'd just closed my eyes when I heard Carol calling. "It's seven. Let's go. Tonier, Bridget! Get up." With that our bedroom door flew open. Bridget stumbled up and headed down the hall to the bathroom, but I didn't move. Carol came over to the bed and pulled down the blanket I'd pulled over my head.

"Neen. I know you just got in, but you going to school. Get your behind up. I'll talk to you about this later." I had hoped I'd made it in before she realized I wasn't in the house. I should've known Carol would realize I hadn't come home. Unlike Barbara, she tried her best to keep up with what was happening with me and Bridget. I loved Carol, but she wasn't my momma. And I was going to tell her so.

That evening I managed to avoid Carol before I had to go to work. After my shift was over, I told Keith and his sister I had to go home, so we only drank a couple of pitchers of beer before Keith took me home. Since Carol and Rabbit usually went to bed around 9:30, I thought I'd successfully avoided her again; I was wrong. When I opened the door, she was sitting in the dark watching *Channel 13 News*.

"Hey, we need to talk. Come sit down." She looked and sounded so much like Mil. It was strange that I'd never noticed the resemblance. For an instant, I felt so ashamed. Carol and Rabbit had taken me in when my own mother didn't want to be bothered with me. And here I was causing trouble in their house. As usual, however, I copped an attitude.

"I ain't got nothin' to say," was my reply. What I really wanted to tell Carol were all the things I had tried to wipe out of my heart by drinking, but I couldn't tell her those things, so I got an attitude. Carol didn't seem to notice. She was so nice. When I was a little girl I used to always look up to Carol. I thought she was sophisticated. She was married with a good husband, who had a job. I used to say, "I want to be like Carol." But tonight she was about to get on my nerves.

"Well, I want to talk to you. Sit down." I flopped down on the far end of the sofa. Carol kept talking, "Tonier, I know I'm not your mother, and I know it's not been easy for you kids. I know that. All I want to do is to be your friend. You my flesh and blood. I know it's hard, but I'm doing the best I can to make sure you and Bridget have a roof over your head. I know it's what Mil would want." She smiled when she mentioned my grandmother. I felt a tug in my chest. Then she continued. "All I'm saying is, I want to do my best by you and Bridget. Rabbit and I want you here. This house is your home." Then she just stopped and stood up.

I wasn't quite sure what to do. She said good night and went to the bedroom she shared with Rabbit. I sat there in the dark for a few minutes. I wanted to please Carol and Rabbit. I didn't want to disappoint to them. I wanted to go back to doing well in school. I promised myself that I wouldn't drink anymore. And so I found myself doing something I'd not done in a long time. I found myself repeating those Bible verses I'd learned at First Baptist Church. I even said the prayer when I got into bed. I was going to quit drinking! I was!

And I kept my promise for about two weeks. Then one night I closed the pizza parlor, and Keith came over. We drank some pitchers of beer before we went over to his mother's house, where we drank some more. I didn't make it home that night either. Carol didn't say anything after that first time. She just sort of gave up on me, like everyone else had, and I gave up on myself. Why bother?

Although I'd had a hard childhood, I still dreamed. I dreamed of being out of the projects. I dreamed that one day I'd meet a handsome man and we would get married, have some children, and live in a nice house. In my dreams, my house was always clean, and there was food in the refrigerator. My husband was tall and handsome. All of the other women would be jealous of me. Our house would be a big two-story house with a basement apartment for Barbara, so she could live with us and not have to pay rent. We'd have four children—three boys and a little girl. Our boys would be athletic but smart. And our daughter would be pretty with long hair. She'd be so beautiful, with lots of friends who would come over to our house for parties. My husband would have a good job. He'd be either a lawyer or a doctor, and I'd be a housewife. We'd spend our vacations in New York in the finest hotels. I'd drive a nice car, and my husband would love me and our children. That was my dream, but it surely wasn't my life.

CHAPTER 4

The Fairy Tale

I am my lover's, and
my lover is mine.

—Song of Solomon 6:3

By the time I was sixteen, I'd dropped out of school, I was a functioning alcoholic, and I was miserable. I wanted somebody to love me. I wanted someone to protect me. I wanted to belong, but I didn't. Even though I still lived with Carol and Rabbit, I felt alone and isolated. Deep inside me was a place that I hid. It was where the real Tonier lived. In that place I kept how the real me felt. She had a voice and could defend herself. I kept that place well hidden from everyone, including myself. Because if I admitted that I was miserable, if I admitted I was afraid, if I admitted I wanted to be loved, then the reality that I was none of these things became real. I pushed those feelings into that deep-down place and put a tight-fitting lid on it. Since there were no fairy godmothers coming to the projects in Annapolis, Maryland, I lived the life I was given.

That meant working full-time at the Emporium Pizza Parlor and spending time drinking with Keith. Somewhere along the way, Keith became interested in me beyond just being drinking buddies. I wasn't sure why. I don't know if it was interest or lust. I didn't know the difference. I'd been abused by men, but none had seemed interested in me beyond the physical act of sex. I'd never had a man who wanted to spend time with me. I'd never had a man pay attention to me. I'd never had a man interested in me, so I confused his attention for love. And for the first time in my life, I fell in love. At least I thought it was love. I came to depend on Keith. He bought me things. He took care of Barbara, and that made me happy. So I decided it had to be love.

I loved him because he was different. I'd never been around a man quite like him. He was nice to me, respected me, and, most important, he made me feel safe, which was something I hadn't experienced since my grandmother died. Of course, it helped that he was tall and handsome. What girl didn't want a good-looking, six-foot-tall man? Was it possible that he was my Prince Charming? When I looked at Keith Cain, my heart just about leaped out of my chest. He took my breath away. Any woman would've had him, and yet he was actually interested in me. *Me!* I wanted to shout it from the highest building in Annapolis: Keith Cain likes Tonier Johnson!

There was no pressure to have sex. It just happened. But with Keith it wasn't just sex; we made love. For the first time in my short life, I actually wanted it to happen. He was a perfect gentleman. His kisses were real. His touch was nice. He didn't get up and tell me to keep it a secret. He held me in his arms and made me feel protected. The more time we spent together, the more I grew to love him. *Love*, something I never thought I'd feel in my life, was happening to me. It seemed too good to be true. When Barbara realized we finally were a couple, it made her happy that I was with one of her drinking buddies.

I knew then that God had smiled on me. I had a perfect man, and Barbara liked him.

Keith was known in the community. He went to church and people respected him. Finally, I was respected, too, because I was with him. People didn't make fun of me anymore like they'd done when I was in school. Now even grown women envied me. I was so proud. Dreams did come true. My Prince Charming had arrived.

Keith would come over to Carol's house to pick me up, and he'd buy liquor and beer that we'd take to Barbara's. I know she was happy that I had someone who showed her a good time, and, for the first time in my life, Barbara was proud of me. She trusted me with Keith. After a while, we'd go out, and I'd spend the night with Keith. His bedroom was on the main level of the Cain house, and a bathroom was just across the hall. He'd sneak me in. At first he was working on his father's garbage truck, so he'd leave before daylight. I'd just stay quietly in his room while he was gone. When he'd return around 10:00 AM, he'd bring me food. It was amazing that his mom never opened the door to his bedroom, where I lay naked in his bed. One night a week turned into three nights, and, before I realized it, Keith and I were living together in his bedroom at his mother's house.

I was sixteen years old, and, while other girls my age were having Sweet 16 birthday parties, I was living with a man who was seven years my senior. But it was such a good life from what I'd known that I thought I had arrived. I had a man who

loved me—a man who Barbara approved of. It was almost perfect until one morning when I woke up not feeling well.

Waves of nausea swept over me, and I threw up everything I
ate until I was gagging. I didn't know what was wrong with me.
While I'd had many sexual encounters, no one had explained
to me what might happen. My mother hadn't bothered to have
any "mother and daughter" talks with me about the birds and
the bees. And Keith and I didn't practice safe sex. I should've
known it would happen, but in many ways I was still a child,
with a child's mentality. Keith took me to the hospital, where
the doctor told me I was pregnant. I thought Keith would be
happy because we were starting a family.

"Keith," I said, "we gone have a baby!" Now I'd have a family.
More important, I'd have a baby who'd love me because I was
his or her mother. This child would love me like I loved Barbara. And I'd take care of this baby. I wouldn't be mean to my
baby. I'd protect my baby. I wouldn't let nobody hurt my baby.
While I was happy, Keith was withdrawn. I couldn't understand
why. He was always telling me how he loved me. He was always
saying how I was his girl, and now I was going to have his baby.
Life couldn't get much better in my mind. But what I didn't
know then was that my Prince Charming was as afraid of his
mother as I was of Barbara.

Mrs. Cain was so unlike Barbara. From what I knew she
didn't drink or do drugs, and she didn't beat Keith or any of
his sisters and brothers. But Keith wanted to please his mother,

and he was afraid of disappointing her. So it took him a while before he could tell her that I was pregnant. She wasn't happy, but she seemed to accept the fact, or at least I thought she had.

One day I was spending the day with Keith at his aunt's apartment when someone knocked on the door. Keith answered the door, and my father, Oatmeal, my aunt Carol, her friend Catherine, a policeman, and a fireman were standing there.

The fireman spoke first, "Are you Keith Cain?"

"Yeah. What's the problem?" Keith asked.

"I have a Vernon Johnson here who says you are holding his underage daughter, Tonier, against her will."

"What? What are you talking about?" Keith was truly confused. I was confused. I was standing behind him in the apartment looking crazy and scared. Suddenly, I saw before my eyes the people from the Department of Social Services coming to Barbara's apartment five years ago and taking me and my sisters and brothers away. My stomach did a cartwheel. I moved behind Keith and held on to his shirt. My knees were weak, and I seriously thought I'd throw up. Inside my heart was screaming, *Please, Keith. Don't let them take me away! Please, Keith.* But I didn't say anything. I vaguely remember hearing Keith explain that I was not being held, and I was free to leave. There was this roaring in my ears. It kept getting louder and louder. I could barely hear him say that my mother knew where I was.

Finally, I heard Oatmeal's voice above the roaring sound in my head scream, "Neen! Get dressed!" I knew that voice. I knew that sound. I'd heard that sound when I was four years old, and he'd screamed at Barbara as he tried to shove her head down the toilet. I wanted to wrap my arms around Keith's middle and beg him not to let them take me away. *I love you, Keith. Save me. You can beat Oatmeal up! Please don't let them take me away.* My heart pleaded with Keith, but my mouth said nothing. I was afraid they'd take me back to that courtroom, and some judge would take me away from Keith. I stood there, frozen in fear.

After a while, Keith turned around and said to me, "Go ahead and get dressed, Neen. You gotta go with your dad." He seemed so defeated. Now I was really afraid. And for the first time I was angry about what was being done to me. How dare Oatmeal come here and take me away from the only man who'd ever loved me. How dare he come here acting like he knew me or loved me. I didn't know him. He'd never protected me or acted like he loved me. That's what I wanted to say, but I just dropped my head and walked back to the bedroom and got dressed.

I didn't say one word to Oatmeal when we left. I didn't say one word when we got back to the apartment he shared with his girlfriend and her son. I didn't say anything for a long time. To hell with him! *You want to be my daddy? Well, too damn late.* And with that I hated him. I hated him for all the things he'd done to Barbara. I hated him for all the things he'd not done for me and my sisters and brothers. I hated him for embarrassing me, for taking me away from Keith. I hated him because he was my father, and he'd never done a damn thing to protect me or make me feel safe. Now he had the dirty nerve to come and take me away from one of the few safe places I'd had since Mil had died. I hated him in the deepest core of my being. But I said nothing.

"Listen to me, Neen. I don't want you with that man," Oatmeal said when we got back to his house. "Do you hear me? That man too old for you. He just taking advantage of you. What I oughta do is take his ass to court. That's statutory rape." As I sat there watching Oatmeal's mouth move, I couldn't understand anything he was saying. I could hear him. I saw his mouth moving, but what he was saying sounded like he was speaking Spanish or something. I didn't know this man. Yet here he stood, telling me Keith was too old.

I wanted to scream *Too old? Do you want to know about the first man who took advantage of me? Were you there when he raped a nine-year-old girl? Do you know how old he was? Do you know his name? Were you there when all the other men raped me?* Inside me, the other Tonier said these things, but the outside Tonier said nothing because it wasn't going to help, and I was helpless to stop what was happening to me again. So I pushed down those feelings and said nothing because I always said nothing.

Almost as soon as I got to Oatmeal's house I became aware of the beatings. I heard the same voice and the same screaming

I'd heard when I lived with Oatmeal and Barbara. Oatmeal hadn't changed, and he regularly beat his girlfriend, just like he beat Barbara. I was terrified that I was listening to him kill her, just like I thought he'd kill Barbara. There was screaming and shouting, and I was afraid all over again. I wanted Keith; I needed him. I longed for Barbara.

In addition to the fighting between Oatmeal and his girl-friend, her oldest son began using me almost as soon as I arrived. He never raped me but just took advantage, and I was too weak emotionally and physically to stop him. He'd catch me in the hallway, pin me against the wall, and fondle my breasts or slip his hands down my panties. Once he caught me in the bathtub, and he climbed into the tub with me while Oatmeal and his mother were having a big fight. I didn't care. I just lay there, and he had the same kind of sex all the other men had had with me. All of this happened to me under the roof of my father, who thought I was being taken advantage of by Keith, a man who actually loved me. But I couldn't tell anyone. Not even Keith. So I put what happened at Oatmeal's house in that place where all the other bad stuff was, and I kept quiet because the outside Tonier didn't have a voice.

To keep me away from Keith, Oatmeal asked his girlfriend's youngest son to follow me. If I went downtown, he'd follow me. The problem was, he was a terrible spy. One day, I was trying to get away from him, so I ducked around a corner. When he came running to see where I'd gone, I stepped out.

"What d'hell you doing?" I demanded.

He was scared out of his mind. "Whatcha talking 'bout?" he asked. He started backing up.

"You following me like some punk. Yes, I am going to see my man, and you and Oatmeal can't stop me."

"I ain't trying to stop you from going nowhere. I'm going downtown." He sounded stupid just repeating it.

"I tell you what. My man will give you money to leave me alone."

"How much money?"

"I don't know. I'll have to ask him." With that the spy became my confidant and pimp. I'd leave home, and he'd follow me down the street. Then Keith would pick me up, give him five or ten dollars, and tell him what time to meet me, so we could go back to Oatmeal's house together. And I'd spend the day with Keith while Oatmeal's spy went to Burger King.

I didn't stay with Oatmeal long. After about a month, I was tired of being there, of hearing Oatmeal beat his girlfriend, of hearing her cry, and of her son trying to feel me up even though he knew I had a man. So one morning I got up and decided I was going back to Barbara's because I knew she'd allow me to be with Keith. By this time I was so hopelessly in love that being away from Keith made me physically ill. He was my sustenance. I longed for him like an addict. In many ways, my relationship with him was the beginning of my life of addiction.

So I went back to Barbara and Keith, and life settled back to normal. Then one day while Barbara and Keith were drinking, he said, "We ought to git married." Barbara laughed and said that would teach Oatmeal. If we were married, Oatmeal, Carol, a fireman, a policeman, not even a judge could take me away from him. So just like that it was settled that I would marry Keith, and everyone thought it was a good idea.

Life was happening. I was just there. I had no idea what being married meant. I had no standard for being a wife. I didn't know how to be a wife, but I was excited about being Keith's wife. Sure, I knew how to have sex with a man. I knew how to be in the house with him, but I had no idea what it meant to be a wife. Yet on October 29, 1985, while I was still a minor, Barbara signed the marriage license, and three days later I legally became Mrs. Keith Cain. For the first time in my life, I knew where I belonged, and I belonged to someone who actually wanted me. I had a place, I was married, and I had a good-looking husband who loved me. And I was seven months pregnant.

When Keith's father heard that we were married, he agreed to pay for a church wedding. I didn't really care. I just wanted to be with Keith, but Mr. Cain insisted. He said we couldn't just get married without a proper wedding. When we started to protest that we couldn't afford a real wedding, he insisted, "Naw. Um gonna give you and Keith a wedding. All you gone have to do is show up. I'll pay for everything. Just show up at the church on Saturday." Most girls would've been ecstatic. Here was Mr. Cain offering to pay for a wedding. The Lord knew Keith and I didn't have any money, but I was numb. I didn't care about a wedding.

Keith's father owned a garbage company. In the daytime, he hauled garbage, but at night, he was known as one of the biggest drug kingpins in Annapolis. So, of course, he couldn't have his son marrying a girl from the projects in a courthouse wedding. Aside from picking my dress and choosing a dress for Barbara, I had little input into our wedding. I did ask Ann to direct the wedding, which she did. This whole wedding planning thing was over my head, and it had to be pulled together in three days. I'd never been to a church wedding, let alone planned one!

Ann helped me pick colors. I decided on navy blue and white. She helped me find a dress that hid most of my pregnancy. I was fortunate that I didn't have a really big belly. Barbara said I carried the baby in my breasts. I didn't know exactly what that meant, but I did know that my chest went from a 32B to a 36DD. My breasts were big and tender all the time. I asked my sister Bridget to be my maid of honor, and my little sister, Shannon, to be the flower girl. And although my colors were blue and white, we bought Barbara a beautiful yellow dress. By the end of the reception, she'd look like a big beetle. She'd be lying on her back on the sidewalk with her legs in the air, but during the wedding, she was beautiful.

True to his word, Mr. Cain provided everything. The church was beautifully decorated with flowers and candles. Although I'd been to Second Baptist United Methodist Church before, I was seeing it for the first time. I'd never seen white roses in the winter or candlestick holders that looked like fans. White bows were at the end of the first three pews on both sides of the center aisle, and he'd hired an organist and a woman to sing. He hadn't forgotten a single detail. A white stretch limousine picked me up before the wedding and delivered Keith and I to the reception.

I remember thinking, *I'm dreaming again*. I was afraid that at any moment someone would call my name and I'd wake up in Barbara's hot apartment. But I didn't. On one side sat my family. Barbara's sisters and brothers were there. Ann and her sister Janice were there. Across the aisle was Keith's family. When I peeked in the church before the ceremony, I remember thinking how different Keith's family looked from mine. You couldn't help but notice. His mother looked like one of those people from *Ebony*. She came in wearing a very expensive-looking dress, and all the women on his side of the church had on expensive-looking clothes. Even the men looked perfect, all dressed in suits and ties. It was clear that Keith's family was well-to-do, while my family members came from the wrong side of town. It was the first time, but not the last, that I'd realize how different Keith and I were.

Like most brides, I wore a long white gown and veil. I was so beautiful, although my belly was noticeably sticking out.

When Rabbit walked me down the aisle, I felt like a princess. And when the minister asked me if I took Keith Cain to be my "lawfully wedded husband to have and to hold 'til death do you part," I smiled and said, "I do." So on the day after my birthday, I became the wife of Keith Cain, in front of our families in a church and, most important, in the eyes of God.

After the wedding, the limousine took us to the Eastport Terrace Recreation Center, where the reception was held. As we rode into that complex, I remembered all the good times I'd had in this housing project when I lived with Mil. The thought of her made me long to see her and for her to know that finally I was with someone who'd take care of me. I looked at the sidewalks where Tia and I used to play, and I wondered where Tia was. Then I saw the Rec Center, and I remembered something I'd never told my grandmother: how the center director had fondled me when I was a little girl. All these thoughts made me happy yet sad at the same time.

When Keith and I arrived, Ann was upset. She wanted the reception to wait for the announcement of the wedding party before people started eating and drinking. But Mr. Cain had said, "I paid for a party. Let's party." And the party had started by the time we arrived. Mr. Cain had really outdone himself. Everything was first-class and plentiful. There was an abundance of food and an abundance of free alcohol. Members of my family, including Barbara and her friends, were enjoying themselves. Free beer, wine, and liquor meant eat and drink until you are either passed out or were put out. The wilder Barbara's friends got, the more uncomfortable Keith's family seemed. Eventually, most of his family left, and the real party started. The DJ was popping, and the freaks were getting their freak on. At some point in the evening, even I couldn't take the celebration. I remember hiding in the bathroom with my head against the cold wall.

After the wedding, life as Mrs. Keith Cain was all that I'd hoped. I had a home, and Keith had invited Barbara and my three younger sisters to come live with us. I'd finally proved to Barbara how much I loved her. I provided her with a place to stay. At first things went well. Keith and Barbara really got along well. They'd drink beer and liquor together. We had a great family! I thought we'd finally put aside all the missed years. I was wrong.

One afternoon, I looked out the window and saw my husband sitting in his truck with his father. They were just sitting there, so I went out and invited them to come in. I noticed that Mr. Cain didn't say anything, and Keith acted like something was wrong. Before I could ask what was wrong, two police cars drove up. One of the officers walked up to the side of the truck where I was standing.

"Keith Cain?"

"Yeah."

"I'm Officer Broomfield. Which of these apartments is yours?"

"201A."

"Okay. Please remain in your vehicle until we've executed the eviction." With that statement, Officer Broomfield walked toward our apartment door. I finally found my voice, but it wasn't really my voice. It just seemed to come out of my mouth.

"Keith! Keith!" I heard myself screaming. I saw myself falling on the ground because my knees wouldn't hold me up. I felt my husband picking me up. I felt myself being carried into the apartment. I saw Barbara cussing. I saw the policemen just standing there. I saw Mr. Cain. But I couldn't move or stop what was happening. Barbara and my little sisters were coming out of the apartment with their clothes in a plastic bag. It seemed like I was in a movie, but the action was happening around me.

Then I was sitting alone in the apartment with my new husband and his father. I think Mr. Cain was the first to speak. I don't really know. I just remember hearing him talking to me and Keith. I felt stupid, and I'm pretty sure I looked stupid. I was pregnant. I was angry. I was disappointed. Once again, they were doing things to me, and I was helpless to stop it.

"You done the right thing. Neen, you and Keith need to be a family. Y'all fixing to have a baby. Yo' mama don't need to be living with you." I wanted to ask him how he knew this. How did he know anything about Barbara or me? Did he know that I loved Barbara? Did he know I was proud to be able to provide a place for her and my sisters? Did he know that for the first time in my life Barbara was proud of me? Did he know I was little more than a child? Did he know how people had always done things to me? He didn't know nothing. I wanted to say, "Shut up! You don't know nothing about me or my family," but I sat there in silence. I wanted Barbara, Shannon, LaTonya, and Tyra. I wanted us to be a family again. I wanted Barbara and Keith to sit in the living room and drink beer.

"Neen, you hear Daddy. Say sumptin.'" My husband looked at me, and at that moment I saw my husband in a different light. Before this time, Keith had been my knight in shining armor. He'd made me feel safe. He'd given me respect in the community. He'd taken care of Barbara. He'd let me fulfill my dream of making my mother proud of me. As we sat there with his father, I saw a man who wasn't thinking about me. He looked like all the other men who'd taken advantage of me.

All I could think about was Barbara and my little sisters. Where would they sleep that night? I couldn't understand why Keith had been so mean-hearted. He reminded me of that judge long ago, who'd taken us from Barbara. Once again a man was taking me away from Barbara. He knew she didn't have any place to go. It bothered me that he brought his daddy to put Barbara out of our home. At that moment I hated Mr. Cain, and I didn't really know him. And I hated Keith for allowing his father to dictate our lives.

After that our life was strained. I didn't want Keith to touch me. One day I came into the room, and he was talking on the phone. When I asked who he was talking to, he pushed me away. So I grabbed for the phone. He pushed me away, but he punched me in my side. When I wouldn't move, he kept punching me. It felt like the day Barbara had punched me with the butt of that butcher knife when I thought she was stabbing me. It didn't hurt much, but it surprised me. It was the first time Keith hit me. It was the beginning of the hitting.

When the New Year began, I was married and very pregnant. One afternoon I was in the bathroom when I noticed a slimy, bloody discharge. I had no idea what it was, so I screamed. Luckily, Keith was still at home. He came running into the bathroom. I said, "Keith! Something is wrong with the baby. I'm bleeding." I didn't know what was happening, but I knew I shouldn't be bleeding. Keith had no idea what to do, but he'd seen Barbara earlier going into the rental office at the complex, so he went to get her. When he came back, I was still in the bathroom. I was crying because I thought I'd done something wrong, and now I was about to lose the baby.

Barbara asked me what had happened. When I explained, she laughed and said, "Your plug just come out. You 'bout to have a baby." As soon as she said that, the pains seemed to begin. No one had prepared me for the kind of pain I was experiencing. I was not ready for this kind of pain. Barbara seemed scared; Keith was as scared as I was. In between contractions, I was crying and begging God to please help me. I remember at one point, when I was really screaming, Barbara came over and said, "Neen! You ain't the first woman to have a baby. Just push when the pain gets bad."

She was right. I did exactly as she said, and at 6:57 PM on January 23, 1986, I pushed Keith Cain Jr. into the world. He was so little, but so beautiful, and he was mine, all mine. There are no words to accurately describe how I felt when I looked at my son. Finally, I had someone who would love me like I loved Barbara, someone who would always love me. Unlike being a wife, being a mother was easy for me. It may have been because of all the practice I'd had with Barbara's children. I don't know, but I loved that little boy so hard, it hurt. And I vowed to be to him all of what Barbara had not been to me.

By the time I went home from the hospital, Keith had invited Barbara and the kids to move back in with us. His excuse was that she could help me with Lil Keith. In reality, he missed his drinking buddy. They now spent endless hours drinking together. She didn't really help me because she was out of the apartment and gone most of the time. I learned by trial and error what to do for Lil Keith.

When my husband wasn't drinking with Barbara, he'd want me to go clubbing with him. Before I learned the term or what it meant, I'd become Keith's trophy. He'd buy me sexy outfits that he insisted I wear when we went out. Most of the clothes he bought were tight skirts and revealing tops. Then we'd go to a bar, and I'd sit on a stool so people could see me.

If a man seemed interested in me, Keith would explode and start trouble. I always thought it was strange that everyone in the neighborhood bars knew that I was underage, but no one questioned my being there and drinking.

One night he wanted to go to dinner after we'd been to a club. I didn't want to go. It was late, and I wanted to go home. I was tired of being Keith's possession. I remember arguing with him all the way to the restaurant. When we arrived, I was determined to go home, so when I got out of the truck, I started walking in the direction of our apartment. I remember Keith calling after me, "Where d'hell you going, Neen?"

I shot back over my shoulder as I continued to walk away, "Um going home. I told you I didn't want to come." I don't remember if it was the cold or what, but I was tired. I should've known what was coming from the tone of his voice. I ignored it. This night I was going to stand up for myself, so I kept walking.

"I said where in d'hell do you think you going?" With that Keith came running across the parking lot behind me. He grabbed me. He was breathing hard, and even in the dark, I could see this look in his eyes. "Bitch, I said where you going?" He pulled me behind a wall. It was Keith's hands around my neck, and Keith who was slapping me. It was Keith who threw me on the pavement and started stomping on me. It was Keith on top of me punching me in the face. It was Keith, but it felt like Barbara beating me in the middle of the street in Meade Village Housing Project because I wanted to go to school.

I don't remember how long the beating went on. I didn't try to run or fight back. I didn't scream. I just lay there because I couldn't believe this was happening. This was the man who'd promised to "love, honor, and protect me." Now he was breathing hard, and, with the same hands that held our son, he was slapping me and choking me. This wasn't happening. This wasn't Keith Cain, the love of my life. This wasn't the man who told me, "You are so beautiful. You take my breath away." This wasn't the man who told me, "You are too beautiful to believe," and, "You are too good to believe." This wasn't the man who'd taught me how to make love and not just to have sex. I lay there looking into the eyes of a stranger, and I couldn't react. I was paralyzed by disbelief.

Eventually, this stranger stopped hitting me. He picked up my bruised, beaten body and literally threw me into the truck. Then he drove away as I lay shaking and whimpering in the passenger side of the truck. I sincerely thought he was taking me somewhere to finish killing me. I was too scared to ask him anything. Finally, I realized he'd taken me to his friend's summer house, which was out on the bay. I could hear the sounds of the water. I really got scared because it was so dark and lonely out there. My mind was racing. I was so scared. I was trembling. I thought he was going to kill me and throw me into the bay. What would happen to Lil Keith? What would happen to my baby? Who would tell him about his mama? Would he think I'd left him like Barbara left me? In my mind, I started begging for my life, but no words came out of my mouth. Instead, I heard myself saying, "Yea, though I walk through the valley of the shadow of death." I was shaking and crying and saying in my mind, *The Lord is my shepherd.*

Then, to my surprise, Keith got out of the truck and started to cry. I lay there so scared I almost peed my pants, and now he was standing beside the truck saying, "I don't deserve to live. Neen, um so sorry. I don't know what happened. Baby, please forgive me." I couldn't say anything. I didn't know what to say. I was scared. I was hurt. I was bleeding. I couldn't talk. Then he said, "Baby. I can't live without you, and I don't deserve your love. I'm going to just end it." Then I thought he walked away. I thought he was going to drown himself, and I knew he couldn't swim.

It didn't take me a moment, but in that split second I saw life without him, and I knew I didn't want to be without him, so I screamed with all my might through the pain in my bruised mouth and jaw. I screamed, "Keith!" I managed to sit up and scream again, "Keith!" I couldn't lose another person I loved. I just couldn't. Then there he was standing beside the truck door, but in that instant I knew he'd changed. He looked different.

I don't remember the ride home that night. I do remember that when we got home, we went to our bedroom. He pulled me to him in bed like nothing had happened. And he had sex with me. It was the first time I felt dirty with my husband. The next morning was like nothing had happened the night before. No one seemed to notice my swollen lip and face. Neither Barbara nor Keith said anything about the obvious pain I was in. They ignored it, so I ignored them.

Life at the Cain house now took a different turn. And I began to hear that sound from my childhood. Keith would come home some days and do an inspection of the house. He'd run his fingers across the coffee table top or the kitchen counter. If it wasn't spotless, I'd get a beating. I'd try to please him, but it was never enough. After that first beating, Keith was careful not to put marks on my face. He'd punch me in the side or back. He'd beat my body.

There was a girl who lived upstairs, and we'd talk. She understood when I said I just couldn't do all of what Keith expected. One day she offered me a "remedy" to help me have more energy. She introduced me to crack cocaine. She said the crack would help me get through. She was right. I remember the first time I smoked. I saw myself cleaning, but I couldn't stop. I cleaned our apartment from top to bottom. I cleaned shelves, rooms, furniture, floors, and ceilings. I had so much energy, I even cleaned for neighbors. By the time Keith, Lil Keith, and I moved, I had become good friends with the girl upstairs and her "remedy."

Although I was now the cleanest woman in all of Annapolis, our married life was still wrong. I just couldn't seem to please Keith. He had changed. He grew distant. I wanted to scream,

"Please, Keith. Please don't leave me. I love you. We need you. Keith!" But the old Tonier had come back, and she knew it was meaningless to say anything. So I retreated to the sideline of life and watched my life happen. By the time 1987 ended, Keith had physically left me and our baby. Now I was alone with a one-year-old toddler. I had no money, no education, and a growing drug addiction.

After being on my own for a year, I found myself forced to go back to the only person who would take us in: Barbara. She still lived in the apartment where Keith and I had lived in Boston Height Circle. Living with her was convenient for me. Now Barbara became my live-in babysitter. Our roles had reversed. She was the one caring for my son. I was a mess, but no one seemed to notice. One night I had to get out, so I walked over to the pay phone and called Jean, Ann's sister. I told her I needed someone to watch the baby. To my surprise, she agreed to babysit Lil Keith.

When I left the pay phone, there was a guy from the neighborhood named Mike just kind of standing there. We started to talk, and he offered to give me a ride to Jean's house. What started out as a casual ride turned into us hanging out and eventually having a relationship. Mike was like a breath of cool air after what had happened with Keith. That first night while we were parked at the ballpark having drinks, for some reason I took my clothes off because I thought he wanted the only thing

I knew how to give men: my body. When he told me to put my clothes back on, I was a little offended and a lot surprised.

I remember asking him, "Wassa wrong? You don't like me? You don't think I'm pretty?" I was a little drunk, but I was sober enough to know men don't turn down free sex. There had to be a reason.

His reply really surprised me. He said, "One, I like you very much. I've been watching you for a while. Two, I respect your father, and I couldn't take advantage of his daughter." I was stunned that he knew Oatmeal, and that he respected him. Mike told me he'd worked with Oatmeal at the Naval Academy. That surprised me because, while I knew that Oatmeal worked, I didn't have any idea where and what he did. I'd learned something that night from a stranger.

After that first night, however, Mike quickly moved from being a stranger to being my "boyfriend." He knew I was married but separated from my husband. We spent a lot of time together. When we finally had sex, Mike taught me something that even my husband had not taught me: how to enjoy sex. Keith had taught me how to make love, but Mike showed me gentleness with passion. Mike made sure I was pleased. He made me feel alive. I became a woman with Mike. My life started to return to whatever normal had been before Keith had left.

Then one night Mike was at the apartment when Keith showed up. Supposedly, he had come to see Lil Keith. Mike was a member of the National Guard, and he was dressed in his uniform. Keith stormed into the apartment demanding to know who Mike was and why he was with his wife. Somehow Keith had been told that I was seeing someone else. It didn't matter that he'd left me and his child for more than a year. It didn't matter that he hadn't provided one diaper or bottle of milk for his son. None of that mattered. What was important was I belonged to him. This was the Keith Cain from our clubbing days when he'd challenge any man who looked at me because I was his trophy.

He didn't ask who Mike was or why he was there. He just walked in and said, "Yo! Man, you need to git on up from outa heah. Dis my wife." He just stood there acting like I was his, like he'd not left me and Lil Keith, like he'd given me money to live on.

I was determined to let him know I was no longer his. So I stood up and said, "Naw, he ain't going nowhere. This ain't your house, and I ain't cha damn wife. You git out!" I don't know where that sound had come from, but I felt like I had to stand up for myself. Keith just looked at me like I'd lost my mind. I thought I had lost my mind. Then he looked at Mike, who had stood up. I guess he weighed the cost and realized it was too high because he just stormed out and slammed the door.

Before I could apologize to Mike or gather my senses, Mike said something that completely took me by surprise. He said, "He's right, Neen, I should leave. He your husband." With that he shrugged his shoulders and walked out of the apartment. It wasn't that he was afraid of Keith; he just respected me. That was what he was saying. I just didn't understand it at that point, so I was a little hurt when he left. I wanted him to stand up to Keith and kick his behind, but he just left. Now I was confused and alone.

Mike was no sooner down the stairs than Keith returned. When he walked back into the apartment, I saw that same look I'd seen in that dark restaurant parking lot. I knew what was coming, but I didn't have the will to run. I just stood there, and he slapped me so hard that it made my ears ring. Then, without another word, he sat down on the couch and started drinking. He'd accomplished what he'd come for. He established that I was his, when and whenever he desired. After a while, he just left. He never saw Lil Keith. He never left money for food or support.

Once he'd established himself as my husband, he never showed up again to demand anything of me. I settled back into my relationship with Mike. Then it happened: I missed my period. I was excited. I thought I loved Mike, and now I was going to have his baby.

"Mike, we gone have a baby," I told him one night. I thought he'd be pleased. He acted like he was surprised. I remember him looking at me, and then he said, "You what?"

"I'm pregnant."

"Neen, we can't have no baby." That didn't make sense to me. We'd been having sex. He'd not used condoms. I wasn't on any form of birth control. Even I knew how people make babies, but Mike explained to me that I was still married. He explained that it wouldn't look right for a married woman to have a baby with another man. What would he say to my father? He went on to explain how he respected me, and he respected marriage, and he respected Keith as my husband. I sat there looking at him, completely confused.

"Well, it looked awright for you to screw another man's wife, and you wasn't disrespecting my father when you was crawling on me." I was angry. I didn't understand Mike's way of thinking. In my mind, when a woman got pregnant, whether she was married to another man or not, she had the baby. Barbara had other men and other children after Oatmeal. I don't remember if Mike convinced me that having another baby was wrong, or I just got tired of listening, but I did. Then he said the only way out was an abortion, and I just agreed. I really had no idea what to expect. The way Mike explained it, it would be a simple procedure. We'd go into the clinic, they'd perform the abortion, and we'd go home. It would take a few hours at most. It was painless, and it was performed by licensed doctors. The way Mike explained it, I wouldn't be having a baby. I had no idea of the process or of the pain afterward, but I'd soon learn.

When we arrived at the community clinic, they made me sign a lot of papers, most of which I didn't understand. All I wanted was not to be pregnant anymore. I thought they'd just do some kind of vacuum process. I was wrong. Because I was already five months pregnant, I had to actually go through a delivery. No one told me that until it was too late. They put an IV in my arm and put me in a hospital room. Then the nurse put some kind of drug in the IV, and she inserted a jelly-like substance into my vagina. I thought it was some kind of painkiller. I was wrong again. Suddenly, I was gripped with the worst kind of pain, and I remembered what it had felt like to have Lil Keith. But I wasn't supposed to be having a baby. I was having an abortion.

When I asked the nurse if she could give me something, she calmly replied, "You will have to push the baby out." What baby? This couldn't be happening to me. The nurse put my feet up in stirrups. I was in this haze as I drifted in and out of consciousness. The pain was getting worse. I was having the worst kind of cramps. I remember a doctor coming in somewhere near the end and saying something about being dilated. Then I thought I heard him say, "Push." And I pushed. This went on a couple of times. Finally he said, "Push," and I felt something come out of me. It was a baby. The nurse took it over to a table. I remember raising up on my elbows. I saw them checking it with a stethoscope. I waited to hear a cry, but none came. They dropped a sheet over what had come out of me, and a nurse wrapped it up in the sheet and dropped it into a tall trash bin. Then the horror that I'd killed a person hit me. I started to cry. I was so sorry. I couldn't hold this child as I'd held Lil Keith. I'd never see this child take its first steps. At that point, I realized what I'd done, but it was too late. I'd killed a person. I'd taken a life. I wasn't any better than the drug dealers who killed people for not paying their bills. I was a murderer!

After a short period in recovery, I was in the car with Mike headed home. I remember looking out the window as huge, silent tears ran down my face. I knew that what I'd done was wrong. But I couldn't take it back. I was so sorry. As I cried, I remembered a song we'd been taught at First Baptist, "Jesus loves the little children, all the children of the world, red and yellow, black, and white, they are precious in his sight, Jesus loves the little children of the world." At that moment, I was hoping he loved the child I'd just aborted. I did!

Two days later I was still bleeding profusely, so Mike took me to the hospital. They did a procedure called a D and C where they scraped the lining of the uterus to remove any remaining blood and tissue. It was now really final. I still had Lil Keith, but the abortion killed more than that baby; it killed something inside me. Mike didn't seem to understand. He didn't seem to understand the dull pain that was inside me. I couldn't tell him about the sound when they dropped what had come out of me into that trash bin. I needed to escape the dead pain that was eating inside me. So I turned to the remedy that helped me cope. I turned to drugs, but to get drugs I needed money. I found support in an old family friend.

CHAPTER 5

Hard Times
Prostitution, Drugs, and Jail

Against you, and you alone, have I sinned;
I have done what is evil in your sight.
You will be proved right in what you say,
and your judgment against me is just.

—Psalm 51:4

When Keith left me and Lil Keith, he left us with very little. I had no money, no education, no job, and no prospect of finding work. I had nothing, so I did what young women in my position do. I went to the Department of Social Services and applied for assistance. I was feeling bad about myself. A day didn't pass when I didn't think about the abortion. It ate at my soul. I remember trying to recite those Bible verses I'd learned at First Baptist Church, but I couldn't remember them. I remember wondering if I was so bad that even God didn't care about me. It was a bad time in my life, so I turned to my remedy for consolation.

I still drank, and I'd do drugs occasionally. I had a son who I absolutely adored. He was my delight. I'd hold him and kiss his little face, and he'd pat my face. "Say 'Mama,'" I'd coach him. He'd look at me with his eyes stretched wide and form his little mouth, but out came "Da-Da." I couldn't believe he'd actually said "Daddy." Then I realized I had another problem. I missed my husband. I wanted Keith to hold me. He was a good man. He only got mean when he drank. I liked Mike, but I loved Keith. So I needed to get him back. It was getting cold, so I decided I'd buy him a leather coat as a gift. The only problem was I didn't have any money. The solution for this problem was right under my nose, so to speak.

There was a man in the neighborhood who was known to lend money to people like me. His name was Bailey, and lucky for me he was not only Oatmeal's friend but Oatmeal's brother's brother-in-law. They were in a club called New Breed. He was someone I'd known all my life. That made it easy for me to approach him about a loan. When I approached him, he was standing beside his truck. He recognized me right away. "Neen. You done growed up." I smiled. Then without hesitating, I said that I needed to borrow $125. He looked at me and said, "How you gone pay me back?" I told him I got a check once a month. I remember him looking me up and down, but he reached into his pocket and counted out the money.

When I asked about the repayment plan, he said, "We kin talk about it." I was too naive to know what he meant, but I learned all too soon. Within a week, he came by one afternoon and asked me to take a ride with him. He took me to an office building where his cleaning crew worked. When we got to the building, he pulled up to a back door, unlocked it, and stepped back so I could go in first. Then he closed the door behind us. Before I could turn around, he walked up behind me and wrapped his arms around me in a bear hug. I panicked. I thought he was going to rape me. I was about to scream when he said, "*Sh!*" in my ear. Then he began to grind his body against mine and fondle my breasts. "You a pretty little chocolate doll. And I do lak chocolate. You make me happy, and I'll make it so you can be happy. Kin you do that?" I nodded yes. And in that backroom, we sealed our deal. Sounded like a fair exchange to me. He'd give me money, and I'd give him sex, whenever, whatever, and wherever he wanted. Bailey became my "sugar daddy."

By now, drugs were becoming a way of life, and I became a willing participant because the drugs had started calling louder than the pain, and visits with Bailey soon became frequent. His donations allowed me to take care of me and my son and provided what I wanted and needed most: a way to purchase drugs. Sometimes he'd pick me up and we'd go to a building he cleaned. Sometimes he'd take me to his house. He had this large two-story house, and, while his wife lived upstairs, he lived in the basement. He was good to me. At first the drugs were just something to do, but they quickly became necessary for me to function.

Everything within me was screaming for me to stop. I'd witnessed nameless people from the neighborhood battling drugs. I'd seen girls I'd grown up with die. I knew doing drugs was wrong. But I was empty inside, and the drugs filled that space with numbness, so I rationalized it by saying it gave me a way to dull the continual pain from what I'd done—and I could always stop.

What I was not able to admit was that I liked what I was doing. So when I heard the warnings about drugs, I thought they were ridiculous. I remember watching a commercial that showed an egg being fried, and the man's voice saying, "This is your brain on drugs." I thought that was stupid; the only effect it had on me was it made me want an egg sandwich. I enjoyed the feeling I got from getting high. My brain was fine as far as I was concerned. The drugs wiped out the pain; they took away the memory of the sound of that baby's body being dropped into a waste bin. They took away the pain of Keith leaving.

At first, the drugs numbed me, but after a while, the drugs became another voice. They'd talk to me and call me. They were loud. In my mind, they'd say things like, *Come on, Neen. You'll feel better. We know what you are going through. We got your back.* There would be days I could resist them, and other times when their call was too loud to ignore. The drugs made promises. The drugs understood when no one else did, including Mike. So I kept looking for drugs.

Finding drugs in the projects was like finding sand at the beach. You knew who to ask, and you knew the price. After the first couple of times, the dealers all knew you. They knew what you could and couldn't afford. They knew when your check was coming in case you said, "Lemme hold sumptin' 'til my check come." Everybody knew I was using. Mike knew it, but he wouldn't let go. I guess he really did love me. At least he'd convinced himself that he did. He'd follow me. He'd beg me to stop, and I'd promise I'd stop. I'd swear this was the last time. I wasn't going to do it again. But I couldn't stop, so I learned how to dodge him. If he found a crack house where I went to smoke, I'd find another.

One night I remember coming out of a crack house, and Mike was waiting outside. He grabbed me and shoved me up against his car. I was high and enjoying a great buzz. He was the last person I wanted to see.

"Neen? What d'hell you doing? What about Lil Keith? You better than dis. Don' you know I love you?" he said as he stood in front of me with his arm just above my head on top of the car. I remember being really spazzed. By this time I was not just smoking crack, I was shooting up.

I looked at Mike. I knew it was Mike, but the drugs spoke to me and said it was Bailey, and he wanted payment. So I reached over and tried to rub his crotch. Instead of leaning in to it like Bailey always did, this person shoved my hands away and screamed in my face. "Whatcha think you doin'?" Hell, I knew what I was doing. I was having a good time. I was going to give him some good time, and he'd give me some more money so I could continue having a good time.

I tried to explain, "Why you mad, baby? Neen kin fix it. Come on, lemme make you feel good." I reached out again, but that made him madder, and, before I realized what was happening, he pulled off his belt and started to beat me like you would a child. I didn't really care. I just held up my arms to keep the belt from hitting my face. The drugs were speaking louder than the beating, so I just took it. After a while, I think he took me home. When I woke up the next morning, I vaguely remembered either Mike or Bailey hitting me. I did eventually remember it was Mike.

Sometimes when Mike came looking for me, I'd hide. Sometimes he'd find me, beat me, and take me home. But I could never tell Mike that I heard him say "I love you." I couldn't tell Mike that I appreciated the fact that he still believed in and wanted me. I couldn't say anything because the drugs would call me. They'd scream in my head, and I couldn't turn them down. After a while, he got tired and stopped looking for me. And I kept visiting Bailey, because not only did I need money for me, Lil Keith, and drugs, but I had to support Barbara as well.

I was still living with Barbara and regularly providing sex for Bailey when I found out I was pregnant. I knew I'd have this baby. I couldn't live through another abortion. I knew it was Bailey's baby, but I never told anyone, not even him. When my second son was born, I named him Brandon. This time there was no husband in the delivery room to tell me how beautiful I was or how much he loved me. There was just me and my baby. That's what Brandon was—my baby. I knew his father. All I had to do was look at Brandon, and I could see his father's face. I didn't need a blood test or DNA. "Mama's baby—Daddy's maybe." A mother just knew. I knew.

Life was really different now. I had two children whom I loved. It was hard to believe that Lil Keith was already two years old. They became my reason for living. I loved those boys! I'd play with Lil Keith, and he'd squeal as I chased him around the apartment. And Brandon was the happiest baby. He didn't fret or cry unless he was hungry or wet. Out of all the things that I'd done wrong, they were what I'd done right. I enjoyed being a mother, although I didn't know anything about being a "good" mother. I enjoyed holding them and kissing their little faces. I'd look at them and remember how it had felt when they were inside me. They were mine, and I knew I'd protect them always! It's what mothers are supposed to do. The only problem was, I didn't have the money to provide even the basics for my sons. I was depressed.

One day I went to the only safe place I knew. I went to Ann's house. By this time, I'd become the worse kind of liar. I lied to myself. I said I was just going to visit Ann. I convinced myself I just needed to talk to her because she'd understand, and she wouldn't judge me. That's what I said, but I ended up stealing some of her checks. I was stupid enough to make the checks out to myself after I forged her name. I was desperate for money for me and Barbara. Since she was taking care of the boys when I was out on the street, I had to help her pay the electric bill and buy food. Even in my drug stupor, I still wanted to help care for Barbara.

I don't know if Ann pressed charges or not, but writing those checks led to my first arrest. When the court case was heard, Ann didn't testify. I was found guilty and given probation before judgment (PBJ) for one year. They explained that once I completed my probation, the charges would be dropped. I was so ashamed. I'd taken advantage of one of the few people who'd given me genuine love and tried to help me. And what had I given in return? I'd stolen from her. She'd taught me how to be a woman, opened her home to me, and introduced me to God, and I'd repaid her by stealing her hard-earned money. I was so ashamed I could barely lift my eyes in that courtroom and look at her. I vowed I wouldn't do anything like that again, but it was just the beginning of my involvement in the criminal justice system.

The expression "The road to hell is paved with good intentions" described me. I had the best of intentions. When I dodged the bullet of jail time, I promised myself and everyone who would listen that I was through with drugs and alcohol. I intended to keep that promise. I was wrong. I kept doing drugs, and, because I'd be high, I'd forget to keep my appointments with my probation officer. As a result of this violation, I was sent to a court-ordered twenty-eight-day program called EXCEL. This was my first involvement with rehabilitation and counseling.

The EXCEL program was divided into two parts: short term and long term. The long-term part of the program used a technique that breaks the spirit and then rebuilds it. I had a sexual relationship with another client named Earl from Clinton. He was in the long-term program. When it was discovered that we were having a relationship, they made him walk around in a tuxedo because they thought he'd preyed upon me. I saw them make people wear diapers or signs.

I was in the short-term part of the program. There wasn't much rehabilitation. They'd ask me a lot of questions and then check the box. No one ever asked me about what happened to me. After telling them about my life of sexual abuse, I was assigned to a male counselor. Somehow, I made it through the twenty-eight days and graduated.

After my first week of sobriety, I participated in an aftercare program. The first meeting was held on a Sunday in Baltimore City. I remember catching a ride with a guy I knew from the neighborhood. People were so encouraging at that meeting. They told me things like "Keep coming back" and "Don't stop before the miracle." They complimented me on how I looked. It was great, and I was encouraged to really do this. The second week was even better. I'd been clean for two whole weeks despite the fact that I'd returned to the same neighborhood. It was miraculous.

When the meeting was over, I was sitting outside on a bench when one of the drug counselors, Mr. Bow, came out. I knew him, so I wasn't concerned or frightened when he offered me a ride back to Annapolis. I got into his car feeling pretty good about life. For once in many months, I was not hearing drugs or smelling fear. All was well. I was headed home to my boys, excited about what tomorrow would bring. I guess I wasn't paying attention. When I looked up, he'd pulled down a dirt road and stopped.

Then I saw it, but too late. He grabbed me, and when I resisted, he threatened to hurt me. "You like it rough. I can do rough." With that he not only raped me, he took away my chance, my hope, my trust, and my opportunity. He violated me in the worst possible way. I trusted him; he represented the establishment and society. He was a *counselor* at EXCEL. He was in the business of *helping* people. When he'd finished, he threatened that if I told anyone, he'd deny it. And who would people believe: a drug counselor or a crackhead? So I pulled up my pants and went back to the only thing that always had my back: drugs.

I stopped going to aftercare. That was a violation of my sentence, so I was sent back to jail for seventy-two days. What amazed me was that no one ever asked me why I lived the way I did. Everyone just assumed that I was not strong enough to resist drugs and alcohol, although I'd been clean for two weeks. They reached conclusions about me. Didn't they see how well I had been doing? I felt like that little girl standing in the bathroom crying during recess. Why didn't Mrs. Moore ask me why I was in there? Why didn't she ask why I came to school stinking and dirty? Then I remembered: Mrs. Moore didn't care, and neither did the counselors at EXCEL. None of them really cared.

I didn't slip back into the old life; I was pushed. I didn't want to go back. I wanted to be a good mother. I wanted to be

clean. I decided, *If they think I'm bad, I won't disappoint them.*
I didn't go back willingly, but I wasn't strong enough to escape
my old life.

When I got out of jail, I went back to my old life because I
had no other place to go. I was still fairly clean, and I looked
great. It wasn't long before I caught the attention of a local drug
dealer. I remember the first time I met him. I was at a club and
he was there with his posse. He always traveled with two or
three guys who drove him around. That night I was looking
exceptionally good. He came over and asked if it was safe to
buy me a drink. I looked at him, and I liked what I saw. He was
very nicely dressed. So I said, "Safe?" He said, "Yeah. I won't
have to bust a cap in nobody 'cause you they lady." I laughed,
and we started a conversation that lasted until the club closed.
That night he just took me home, but we did some deep throat
kissing and feeling in the back of his car.

The next Thursday night, I purposely showed up late at
the American Legion. He was waiting for me. So we started
hanging out. And although I knew he was married, I became
his "girlfriend." I later learned that, while I was his Thursday
night special, there was at least a Monday blue plate special and
possibly others. I didn't really care at the moment. He'd spend
the night with me at Barbara's apartment, or we'd go to a hotel.
When he'd leave on Friday morning, he always left me a big bag
of powdered cocaine. I'd never snorted cocaine before, but my

"Boo" taught me, and I learned quickly. Now I was an alcoholic who smoked crack and snorted cocaine.

Being a dealer's girlfriend pretty much kept me off the streets. It gave me time with my boys. One thing I was determined to be was a good mother. While Brandon didn't have a father of record, he had me. He'd always have me. Lil Keith, however, had a father, and whatever else Keith Cain was not, he was an attentive father. Our deal was that Keith would take Lil Keith on the weekends. Usually, he'd pick him up after work on Friday, and I'd pick him up on Sunday. By this time Keith Sr. was dating someone. I didn't particularly like her, but I didn't have much say about where he took our baby. I didn't want any other woman to pretend even for a weekend that she was Lil Keith's mother. I was his mother. I was proud to be his mother.

I was really surprised when I came home one Friday and Barbara told me that Keith had already picked up the baby. I had this feeling that something was wrong, but I dismissed it. Even when I felt the familiar fear creep up on me, I pushed it aside. That weekend seemed to drag on forever. When Sunday came, I walked over to Keith's apartment to get my son. He was not at home, so I asked around until somebody told me where his girlfriend lived. When I got to her apartment, there was my son riding his Big Wheels and having a good time with this other woman. Something pulled on my heart. I wanted to scream at her, "This ain't your child!" But I didn't say it. Instead, I said, "I come to get my son."

She looked me up and down like she was inspecting something from the gutter. Then, real nasty, she said, "And you are who?" She knew who I was. That really pissed me off.

So I looked right back at her and said, "Um his mama. Tonier Cain." I seriously wanted to slap the daylights out of her.

"You gon' have to wait 'til Keith come back," she said.

I said, "Naw. I ain't got to wait on Keith. Um taking my son."

"Well, you gon' have to wait 'til I call Keith." It wasn't what she said; it was her whole attitude. She didn't even invite me in but instead closed the door in my face. *Who did she think she was?* Then she came back from the phone and said, "Keith said you can leave, or I should call the police. He didn't really care which but you can't take Lil Keith."

It hit me then what was happening. They were doing it to me again. I was losing control. Life was happening to me. Then I got really mad. "Naw hell. You ain't gone tell me when I can't get my child. Open this damn doe, bitch!" I started beating on the door and screaming. I couldn't see or hear my child, and I started imagining all kinds of things. I guess she did what Keith told her to because, within a few minutes, two police cars with four policemen showed up. By this time, I was good and hot. She wasn't going to tell me what I could and couldn't do with my son. She didn't even know me. I was pretty upset, and we were both screaming at each other.

I remember this one policeman saying to me, "Ma'am, you are going to have to calm down, or I'll have to put you in handcuffs." *You will have to do what?* I thought. I could hear the other policeman having a conversation with *that* woman. I heard her telling him about how I was a "crackhead," and the father didn't trust me with our son. I heard it. Just like I'd heard that judge a long time ago talking to Barbara ("You are unfit to care for these children"). I heard it, but I wasn't going to let happen to me what had happened to Barbara.

Finally, the two policemen talked to each other while I just stood there and stared at Keith's girlfriend. I know she could see the hate in my eyes. Then one of them said to me, "Here's the problem. Keith Cain Sr. is not here to verify custody. This lady says she is keeping the little boy for his father. This lady says she bought all these clothes this child has on, and she is refusing to allow you to take any of the clothes. So here's what we are going to do. You go back home and bring clothes for the child. Then you will be able to take your son." I couldn't believe they'd believe this lying woman, but I had no choice. They told me to go get clothes and come back. As I walked away, I remember seeing the policemen still talking to her, and something inside my head said something was wrong. *Don't leave*, a voice inside said, but I was sober, and the sober me did what she was told.

I didn't walk back to Barbara's apartment—I ran most of the way. I collected some clothes for Lil Keith and ran back across town. When I turned the corner, the first thing I noticed was that the police car was gone. I remember saying out loud, "I hope that bitch don't start nuffin' now." I stopped to collect my breath before knocking on the door. I knocked. No one answered. I knocked again. No one answered. Then I got scared. I started calling her name and Keith's name. No one answered. The louder I knocked, the more I realized no one was there. There was only a hollow sound, an empty sound. Then I took a deep breath, and I could smell something familiar. It was all around me, and I was terrified. It was fear. Before anyone told me, I knew that my son was gone. I knew they'd taken him.

I was frantic. I called everyone I knew. No one knew where Keith had taken our son. I called Keith's friend Blue. He pretended he didn't know. "Naw, Neen. I ain't seen Keith. You sure Keith took the little man?" I called Keith again and again. Finally, someone told me that Keith had taken Lil Keith to relatives out of state. They'd taken my son! I'd never see my child again. At that moment I couldn't breathe. I didn't want to breathe. The pain of them taking Keith was so much bigger than the pain of anything else. It was bigger than being molested; it was darker than being abused by Barbara; it was heavier than the guilt of the abortion. It closed in on me. It surrounded me. It suffocated me.

I sank into a place so dark I couldn't see daylight. I wanted to die. I wasn't fit to live. I was worthless. They'd allowed Keith to take away my son, and I had no idea where he was or how to go about finding him. For days, I couldn't talk. Even Barbara seemed to know. She helped with Brandon. She left me alone to grieve. And I grieved like a mother who has lost a child. I grieved like a mother who has stood beside the grave of a child who has died. My heart hurt so bad it was painful to touch my chest. I hurt all over. Then one day an old voice inside said, *I can make you feel better. Come on, Neen. I got your back.*

So I turned to the only friend who could help me forget. Drugs became my way out of the pain. In the past, I'd do drugs on the weekends. Now drugs became my life. I roamed the streets looking for that high that would ease the pain I was in. I did more and more desperate things to get high. At first I traded sex for money with Bailey, but now I'd service anyone who'd give me a hit. I shared crack pipes and even dirty needles.

I lived on the streets because it was convenient. And someone was always getting high in the streets. I'd sleep in abandoned houses. Sometimes I'd sleep in crack houses. I was dirty. I smelled. I was disgusted with myself, but I couldn't stop. Every now and then, I'd go to Barbara's apartment to check on Brandon. I loved my son, but the pain was so great. The hurt of having Lil Keith stolen away from me was like a running sore. I now did all the things real addicts did. I was smoking crack, snorting cocaine, and shooting cocaine. I did whatever it took to dull the pain. But it took money to purchase drugs, and I didn't have enough money.

Although I was still receiving a small social services check, I needed more money. I became a prostitute in earnest. I'd become the girl on the corner trying to pick up any man who wanted to use my body. Surprisingly enough, there was usually someone who'd stop and pick me up. I had sex in alleys, behind Dumpsters, in cars, standing up, lying down, on my knees, and any way they wanted. They'd give me some money, and I'd buy some more drugs. I had sex with Hispanic men, white men, black men, Asian men, tall men, short men, bald men, Jews, and Gentiles. Whoever had the money and was willing to pay, I would service. Some of the "tricks" were mean, and, because they were paying, they felt they could do anything to me. I was forced to participate in all kinds of degrading acts. Some of them were brutal. I was beaten. I was abused. Sometimes I was robbed because a man would refuse to pay me. I wanted to stop, but I couldn't. I needed money, and it was the only way I knew how to get it.

One day I was at Barbara's house looking through the belongings from my married life. There were the pictures from my wedding. There I was in my beautiful wedding dress. There was Barbara in that yellow dress. It was all there: the stretch limousine, Keith standing at the altar, Ethel Cain and her family, me and Keith dancing at the reception. It was all there. I was a beautiful bride, but, as I looked at those pictures, I was struck by something. I was not smiling in *any* of the pictures!

Then I found some checks with "Keith and Tonier Cain" on them. I felt as if God had dropped a blessing in my lap. They were our checks, and I decided for survival I'd use them. It didn't matter to me that I was still on probation. I had a pressing need. So I wrote some more checks. I needed money for clothes, food, and living. Of course, sometimes I'd exchange the food and clothes for drugs. I thought the account must've still been open. In some ways, I figured Keith owed it to me. He'd stolen away my child and my happiness. He'd taken my peace of mind. He'd robbed me of raising my son, so I used his money. I had to take care of Brandon. He was mine, and mine alone. So I wrote checks, and eventually I got caught.

In early 1989, I was arrested again. They charged me with passing worthless checks, theft, and uttering. While I was being processed into the detention center, I found out I was pregnant. I was going to have another baby. One visiting day, Barbara brought Brandon so I could see him. I remember being brought up from my cell. When I got to the holding area, there was some kind of mix-up, and the control officer seemed unable to buzz me through. I could look through the glass door and see Barbara and Brandon. As the control officer kept asking the same question, I said to her, "Are you a dumb-ass?" She then announced over the address system, "Cain visit canceled." I was so angry I pushed the officer. That was a big mistake. She pushed the alarm and screamed "10-10," which means officer assistance. Without warning, at least six officers grabbed me and threw me down. Then the same control officer said, "She's pregnant." So they grabbed my legs and arms and carried me to solitary confinement.

When my bail review came up, I was released on personal recognizance. I went back on the streets. I had nowhere else to go. I had a monkey on my back that had grown into a gorilla. I was carrying around all the abuse from my childhood, the rapes and molestation, the broken marriage, the abortion, the stolen child. It was all in there, and it hurt so bad. I couldn't tell anyone. No one seemed to care. All I could do was to continue taking the drugs that dulled the pain. The only problem was that the drugs wore off, and I'd have to get more. I wasn't very good for myself, and I was even less of a mother.

There was no doubt I loved Brandon; I just wasn't a good mother. He was all I had left. But I was afraid of becoming too attached to him. I knew I couldn't provide for him. When Barbara didn't look after him, I'd take him with me in the streets. We were filthy. I learned that people are more sympathetic to a woman with a child than a single woman alone, so I'd take Brandon and panhandle with him. One of my favorite places to stand and beg was the local grocery store. People would pass by and look. I could tell they were disgusted. I was filthy, and Brandon was filthy. It usually worked. Someone would go into the supermarket and then come out and give me a package of Pampers. Sometimes I even got food and change.

I also would go over to this nonprofit organization called Birthright Inc. that provided women like me with clothes and Pampers. One day a short white lady with curly red hair stopped to talk to me. Her name was Kathy. She didn't seem to be put off by how I looked or smelled. I liked Kathy. Whenever I went in for assistance, she was always so friendly and helpful. She looked out for me. She'd give me gift certificates, food, or formula for Brandon. She had a kind and gentle spirit that made me trust her and feel safe around her.

But I kept doing destructive things. I was smoking crack, snorting cocaine, and prostituting. My life was spiraling downward, and I felt helpless to stop it. So I went along for the ride, and I took Brandon along because I was his mother, and, wherever I went, he went. I was a drug addict with a bigger-than-life addiction, and now I was about to bring yet another life into this world. This time I had no idea who the father was. It could've been any of the many tricks who supplied money to fund my lifestyle. My drug-dealing boyfriend thought the baby was his. I wasn't sure. I really didn't care. It would be my child.

Although I was pregnant, I didn't allow my pregnancy to interfere with my life. I kept getting high and drinking. On August 13, 1989, I was having sex with a trick when my water broke. I felt this gush of water. By now I was an old pro at having babies, so I said, "Either I just peed on myself or my water just broke." He stopped moving in me, and said, "Huh?" So I repeated myself. He jumped off me and started to wipe himself as he got dressed and hurried out of the room.

"Hey, wait a minute. Kin you take me to the hospital? Um 'bout to have a baby." He threw a ten-dollar bill on the bed and walked out of the room. All I could see was enough money for another hit. So instead of heading for the hospital, I went across the street to a shooting gallery and bought myself a hit. I was in a hurry, but the pusher didn't have any cocaine. So I had to wait while she went out and bought what I wanted, came back, mixed it, and filled an old syringe with the mixture. I didn't object to the used needle. With ten dollars' worth of cocaine flowing through my veins, I was ready to go have this baby. The pusher went across the street and got my john to give me a ride. I was high, and I was barely feeling the contractions.

When I got to the hospital, my vitals were off the chart. The cocaine that had made me numb had also raised my blood pressure and the heart rate of the baby. I was told that the baby was in distress and might die. Hearing the baby could die really struck fear in my mind. I couldn't lose another baby. I couldn't cause another baby to die. I started crying and begging the doctors—"Please, don't let my baby die." People were rushing around doing things to me and making arrangements to transfer me to Francis Scott Key Hospital where they had a neonatal unit.

I was lying there and the pain had started as soon as the cocaine's effects wore off. Because I had cocaine in my system, someone from the ER had called the hospital's social worker. She reminded me so much of Mrs. Lewis, who'd come to Barbara's apartment so long ago and removed me and my sister and brothers. She wasn't a black lady; she just sounded like Mrs. Lewis. "Tonier, I need some information from you, so we can transfer you." I remember just looking at her. The contractions were really starting now.

"Okay. What is your full name?"

"Tonier Deneen Cain."

"Tonier, are you taking drugs?"

That was a stupid question, I wanted to scream.

"How long has it been since you used drugs?"

"An hour ago?" Hell, I couldn't remember.

"What kind of drugs did you use?"

By now, I was screaming. I wanted that baby out of me. Most of what happened after that was a blur. I remember telling her I didn't know the baby's father. Finally, one of the doctors said they had to move me. So I was pushed out of the ER on a gurney into a waiting ambulance for the ride from Annapolis to Baltimore.

Four hours later, at 11:30 PM, I gave birth to my first daughter, whom I named Whitney after Whitney Houston. She was so beautiful and so tiny. She was a preemie who weighed only four pounds at birth. They told me that she was an addict because all the drugs I'd been using were in her tiny body. I was so upset. I hadn't thought about what I was doing to the baby. I remember holding her and promising her that I'd take care of her the rest of her life. Like Brandon, she was mine and mine alone. After three days, they sent me home to Annapolis without Whitney. Aside from the day when Keith had stolen Lil Keith and the day I had the abortion, it was the darkest day of my life. I'd never had to leave a baby behind. I felt like I was forsaking my baby. Besides leaving her behind, I couldn't visit her every day because of the distance. So I made up for not being there by calling collect every day. The nurses were kind, giving me updates on how she was doing.

With Whitney's birth, I realized I had a new responsibility. Now I had a daughter. I had to protect her in ways that I didn't have to protect Lil Keith and Brandon because I knew the dangers of being a little girl without a protector. I had to be her safeguard. Finally, I received a call from the hospital saying I could come take Whitney home. I was so happy. I could finally bring my little princess home. Since my first two children were boys, I didn't have any baby girl clothes. I went out and stole a yellow dress. Tomorrow couldn't come fast enough.

Ten days after she was born, I went back to Baltimore to take my first daughter home. But before I returned to Baltimore, I'd been on the street doing drugs. It was my lifestyle, so the day I went to pick up Whitney, I looked and smelled like a street person. I wanted my baby, but I didn't care enough to clean myself up. No one really cared how I looked. So I patted down my matted hair and put a do-rag on it. After catching a ride, I went to Francis Scott Key Hospital with that yellow dress to get my baby.

I was happy. When I got there, the nurses treated me like a human. If they were disgusted because of how I looked, no one showed it. They told me about caring for the baby. Then they put that stolen yellow dress on my little girl. She was so beautiful. She reminded me of sunshine, so I called her Sunshine. At that moment, I felt like I'd come in from a cold day, and the heater was warming my body. I could feel pride and happiness in my chest. And I promised that I was going to start taking care of my children. I was going to come out of the streets. I was going to get started in a drug program. I was going to be a better mother to Brandon and Whitney than Barbara had been to me and Bridget, Vernon, Terance, and Teli. I was going to be a good mother. On the ride from Baltimore back to Annapolis, I just stared at the baby. That was a good day.

When I got back to Barbara's apartment, I was still high on motherhood. I had two beautiful children. And I was determined not to listen to drugs, regardless of how loudly they called. I was anxious for Brandon to meet his new baby sister. Everyone was excited about the new baby. She was so tiny, but she was so pretty. I was so proud. Despite all the things I'd done wrong, Sunshine was something right. Although I'd poisoned her little system, she'd been given back to me clean. And I was going to keep her clean, and clean myself up. I promised.

As I was showing her off to the neighbors, a police car pulled up. I don't know why, but something inside me said, *It's about to happen again.* Then the policeman and the woman with him were knocking on Barbara's door. She cracked the door like I'd done all those years ago when Mr. Livingston and Mrs. Lewis had come. The officer asked, "Is Tonier Cain here?" I walked to the door with Whitney in my arms.

"Yeah. Um Tonier."

"Mrs. Cain? May we come in?" The whole time he was talking, I was trying to figure out in my mind what I'd done. Was he there about the stolen yellow dress? Had someone from the grocery store complained about me panhandling? Did the hospital call them? What did they tell them? What had I done? I couldn't think straight. I was gripped by this feeling that was taking my breath away. "Barbara, hold my head out of the window. I can't breathe." But Barbara didn't say anything. She just stood there looking confused, angry, and afraid. So I stepped back, and the officer and the woman came into the apartment.

"Ma'am, this is Ms. Cromartie from the Department of Social Services." She just inclined her head toward me. "Mrs. Cain, I have a warrant for your arrest. And Ms. Cromartie is here to take your children into custody." I didn't hear anything else. The sound was deafening. It was roaring in my ears. It was exploding in my head. It was screaming in my face. It was hollering so loudly I couldn't hear my heart beating. I think I started to beg and cry at that point. I remember as the social worker took Whitney from me, I dropped to my knees, screaming and crying, "Pleeze! Pleeze! What I do? What I do?"

Somewhere in the background of this confusion I vaguely remember hearing the officer say the warrant was for passing worthless bank checks. *What? This was because of Keith?* The officer walked behind me at just the moment I fell, grabbed my wrist, and lifted me up as he put the handcuffs on. I tried to reach out for Whitney, but I was restrained. It seemed like the whole apartment had erupted into a huge mass of confusion. Barbara was cussing, my little sisters were crying, and there stood my beautiful little boy crying. When I reached out to him, the officer snatched me up and restrained me. I was yelling at him that my baby needed me. My Brandon needed me. Then the second officer who hadn't moved yet picked up Brandon. Brandon reached out for me and started kicking and screaming, "Mommie! Mommie!"

"Pleeze. Pleeze. Don't take my babies." Neither officer was moved by my pleading. Ms. Cromartie just turned and walked out of that apartment with my heart in her arms. All I could see was that yellow dress. All I could hear was Brandon screaming my name. I remember I couldn't breathe. My head was throbbing. My arms were behind me. I couldn't touch them. I couldn't reach out. Suddenly, I was a little nine-year-old girl, and a drugged-out, drunken man was pushing his tongue into my mouth as he pushed himself into my body. It hurt so bad, but there was no one to stop it. "Please stop. It hurts. Somebody please help me. Somebody make this stop." But no one came to help me.

When they finally got all three of us out of the apartment, they put me in the back of one police car, and the social worker with my two children in the other. By this time, neighbors were standing outside looking and cursing about how it was a "damn shame" that "white folks always taking black children from their mother."

"Mil! Mil! Pleeze help me. They taking my babies. Oh Gawd! Dey taking my babies! Um gone die. Ah can't breathe. Mil, pleeze help me!" I found myself calling for my grandmother. I hadn't done that for a long time, but now I needed Mil, the only person who had consistently protected me. I needed her. She came to me when I tried to commit suicide. I didn't believe in ghosts. I had forgotten about the God I'd accepted at First Baptist Church. I was just willing to try anything to make this situation right. I kept screaming from the backseat of the police cruiser as it pulled away. And despite my screaming, no one came. Not Mil. Not God. No one! Once again, I was alone.

When we got to the jail, the officer pulled me from the backseat and took me to processing, where I had my picture taken and I was fingerprinted. Then I waited for them to process my name and information to determine my security classification. I didn't care. I just sat there. I wanted to die. Inside, I don't know if I was praying or just wishing, but I was saying, *Pleeze, let me wake up. Let this be a dream, like the one I had about Mil when I tried to kill myself.* But I knew it wasn't a dream because the room was filled with other people making noise. This was real, so I prayed or wished to die. *Pleeze, let me die. I don't deserve to live.* I didn't deserve to live. I didn't want to live. They'd taken all my children, first Keith and now the state of Maryland—all gone. I wasn't fit to live. *Pleeze, let me die.* I wondered why I couldn't just die.

I sat there numb and silent. When the nurses asked me questions about my family history, I said "no" to everything. I didn't care. I wanted my children. Why didn't they understand? They'd just taken my ten-day-old daughter and my two-year-old son. Now they wanted to know about my family medical history. I didn't care, and I wasn't going to help them. Eventually, they put me and another girl in a small cell. At first, I didn't pay much attention to the other girl. Then I realized she was sick. Her name was Debra. She had a fever, and her face was swollen. She told me she had high blood pressure. She was groaning and complaining that her stomach hurt. I didn't know what to do, so when they brought us some lunch, I said Debra needed to see the nurse.

Finally, the nurse came to give out medication. When she saw Debra, she said she wasn't sick enough to go to the hospital. It took three of us to lift Debra so she could take her medication. Then it wasn't Debra anymore, it was me. I was four years old, and it seemed like I was back in that tent at Anne Arundel General. No one came to see about me. No one came to ask if I needed help. They were treating Debra the same way, and it made me mad. She needed help, so I called my brother collect from the pay phone in the inmate holding area. I told him to call 911. After three calls, they dispatched an ambulance to the detention center. The next day they took Debra to the hospital for tests, and she went to the medical wing when she came back to the detention center.

It didn't end there. When they removed Debra, I was told I was going to solitary confinement. "Why?" I asked the guard. The officer told me it was because I'd called 911. I was being put in confinement because I'd helped someone. I didn't care. I'd done something nice, and it had cost me. So for fifteen days I was alone with all my fears.

I'd smelled fear, but this time the fears were all very real. I was alone, but I wasn't by myself. That cell was crowded with all my fears and failures. I tried to sleep, but sleep wasn't an escape because, when I slept, all I could hear was Brandon calling me, "Mommie! Mommie!" Then I'd wake up in a cold sweat. When I closed my eyes, I saw my children's faces. I heard their cries. Those fifteen days were awful. If I lay down on my back, I felt those men's bodies holding me down and penetrating me. I couldn't breathe. I was afraid to lie down, so I'd curl up with my knees to my chest. That way no one could force themselves into me. I tried to pray, but I'd forgotten how. I just remember the black. The light was on, but all I could see was black. The black was real. I could feel it. I could smell it. I could touch it. Just when I thought it would swallow me, they came and took me out of that room—but not out of the blackness.

When I went back to my cell, I was told that a woman named Kathy had visited me. This was the lady from Birthright who'd always been so kind to me. My attempt at being a Good Samaritan had made the local newspaper. Not only had someone noticed what I'd done, Kathy had actually come to see about me. Maybe I wasn't so bad. Maybe someone did care about me. I kinda hoped so. Kathy seemed like a nice lady, and she always made me feel safe. I hoped she really did care about me.

CHAPTER 6

Imprisoned

Around midnight Paul and Silas
were praying and singing hymns to God,
and the other prisoners were listening.

—Acts 16:25

When the time came for my court appearance, I was so far down. I didn't really care about where I was or where I was going. That morning the judge was just another part of the blackness that was closing in on me. "Tonier Cain." I stood up when he called my name. The judge looked at me. I could tell he was disgusted. He looked at me like the police officer who'd transported me after taking me away from my children. He looked at me like the policemen Keith's girlfriend had called when Keith stole Lil Keith. He looked at me like I was a piece of trash. And I just looked back because I really didn't care. He was just a part of the blackness.

"Do you know why you are here?" I just looked at him. I must have looked pretty stupid because I didn't answer, and he kept talking. "Miss Cain, I want you to turn around and look at these people seated in the first two rows." When I turned around I saw Carol, James, Dorothy, Jumbo, Sharon, Oatmeal, Ann, Ella Mae, and my family. I wondered why they were there. But it wasn't Carol or the others. It was a group of strangers. "These people are the hardworking folks you stole from when you passed those worthless checks. You knew that account was closed. You knew you were taking something that didn't belong to you. You are . . ." He kept talking, but what I saw were five little children sitting on a bench as someone who sounded and looked like him told a crying Barbara, "I am appalled by your actions. These are your children. Yet, you, Mrs. Johnson, have allowed these children to live in what can only be described as a pigsty. I have looked at pictures taken of the apartment where you left these children, and it is despicable. I have presided over many cases, but I have never seen a case as bad as this."

I came back to the present and the sound of the judge's voice saying, "Writing these worthless checks makes you no better than a rapist. What you have done is rape these people of their hard-earned money. I am going to protect the state of Maryland from you. You will spend the next thirty-three months in the prison system of the state of Maryland. You are sentenced to three months per count. That equals thirty-three months off the streets and without the possibility of afflicting any further harm on these and any other helpless people." I don't remember if he banged his gavel or what. I just remember the officer who'd been standing beside me pulled me back to where the other prisoners were sitting.

The roaring in my ears was so loud I barely remember anything beyond him calling me a rapist. He said I had raped someone. I had raped someone! What about me? What about the men who'd raped me? I was a little nine-year-old girl. I was scared, and I was hungry. But I couldn't let anyone hurt my sister and brothers; they depended on me. So I stood in front of the bedroom door. I felt his hands between my legs. I felt him trying to push something into me. "Stop! Barbara, make him stop." I felt the pain. Make it stop. Make him stop. No one made him stop. I knew rape! *I'd* been raped!

Most of what happened after my court appearance was a blur until I was transferred to the Maryland Correctional Institution for Women (MCIW). I learned what it meant to be stripped of your dignity. I learned what it meant to be dehumanized. I remembered what it felt like to have someone watch you as you showered. The only difference was it wasn't Oatmeal's girlfriend's son coming into the bathroom to touch my vagina and breasts. The officer just squirted some gel in my hands and told me to apply it to all the areas of my body where there was hair. Then she just stood there and watched me shower. After I had showered, I was given the standard prison attire: a pink jumpsuit and a red jacket with the letters MCIW on it.

MCIW reminded me of a college campus, or at least what I thought a campus would look like. The buildings were arranged according to the sentence an inmate had received. All inmates came into Building 192: C Wing was where prisoners were admitted; A Wing was home to women serving life terms; and D Wing was for inmates who were placed in lockdown. Unlike the detention center, MCIW didn't have bars on the cells. Inmates were allowed to go back and forth between buildings while the officers watched from towers. It looked good, but I was afraid most of the time. Things happened at

MCIW that I'd not experienced on the street. I was desperate to get out of prison.

After three months, I wrote a letter appealing my sentence. One thing I learned from the other inmates was how to play the game. I told the court what other inmates taught me always worked. I told the judge I was truly sorry for what I'd done. I told him I'd learned my lesson, and I asked for another chance. It worked, and I was granted a new hearing. I don't think I completely fooled the judge; however, he did grant my release. He warned me, "I'd better not catch you with even a crayon in your hands." I was so relieved. I did promise I'd walk the straight and narrow. I promised. The judge dropped my sentence and put me on probation for the remaining time. Then they released me back to the streets.

There I was again, back in familiar territory. I had no home, no family waiting, no children, no job, no money. I had nothing. I went back to what I knew best. I went back to prostituting for a living because I didn't know anything else. I went back to drugs because they "understood me, and had my back." No one offered me any kind of help. I didn't know where to get help. There was no mandatory twenty-eight-day program, no aftercare. Nothing.

One day while I was looking for somewhere to sleep, I ran into a homeless man named Earl. I'd seen him a few times, but I didn't know him. His hair was in dreads. He looked kind of crazy. We started talking. Earl told me he lived under a bridge.

He showed me his place. He had painted pictures on the wall. Earl understood my being alone, so he invited me to live with him. "You ain't got to be by yo'self. You kin live here." It was nice, so I started living under the bridge with Earl. When we had money, we'd buy crack and get high. Then we'd lie underneath the bridge and listen to the cars. Sometimes, I'd lie on the sand beneath the bridge. I'd wonder about the people passing just over us. I wondered if they knew we existed. I wondered if they knew that just beneath the bridge was another world, or they just didn't care to know. I wondered.

My days consisted of wandering the streets and hustling money in any way I could. I'd steal if the opportunity presented itself. I'd prostitute if a trick would give me some money or drugs. One particular day I ran up on these two guys on the corner of an apartment building. They had a big bag of crack. I saw an opportunity. I went over and got friendly. I said, "I'll do you if you give me five rocks. Watcha say?" We went back and forth for a while. Then we agreed I'd service both of them for ten rocks. We got up and went behind the building. Once we were in the parking lot, however, they refused to share the crack with me. But I still had to service them. After we'd finished, they began beating me. They beat me like Keith had beaten me in that alley behind the restaurant. They stomped on me. They busted my lip. Then they stepped over me and left me lying on the pavement.

I don't remember how long I lay there. When I got up, I stumbled out of the alley. There was a policeman across the street standing beside his car. I started toward him to tell him what had happened when he called my name, "Ms. Cain." I was so glad to see him. I didn't stop to think about why he knew my name or why he was calling out to me. Before I could tell him what had happened in the alley, he said something about a warrant for my arrest and shoved me against his car. As the officer was handcuffing me, the two men who'd just raped me passed by, pointing and laughing. I tried to tell the officer, but he thought I was trying to escape. To restrain me he shoved my head against the car, and, when my head hit the car, my nose started to bleed. Blood shot everywhere.

I found myself back in jail. This time I was angry at the world. I was angry about how everyone continued to do things to me. I was angry that Keith had been able to steal my little boy. I was angry that they had taken my children. I was angry that these two men had been able to rape me and get away with it. I was angry that no one ever asked me what had happened to me. I was angry, so I began acting out. I'd cuss the guards. I wouldn't cooperate. I'd start stuff. Hell, I was mad. All this acting out kept landing me in solitary confinement. I didn't care. I was mad.

The officers tried to ask me questions. When I wasn't being smart-mouthed, I wouldn't answer. "Tonier, we're just trying to help you." I'd tell them to kiss my ass. "Y'all ain't tried to help me when they took my children. Don't tell me 'bout no helping me." They kept asking me questions. I kept ignoring them. I knew they didn't care. No one cared. No one listened. No one was interested in Tonier. I knew this. Since they didn't have any real information about me, they made whatever diagnoses they could. There were no counselors or therapists who actually knew what had happened to me. There was no one qualified to diagnose what was going on, and I wasn't telling. To hell with them. So they concluded I was crazy, which wasn't far from the truth. But being crazy didn't begin to describe what was going on with me. What it did was allow the jail's doctor to prescribe medication to keep me calm and out of their way.

It was in jail that I was first given psychotropic medication. They gave me Thorazine for psychotic behavior, Ativan for anxiety, and Lithium to help manage what they called bipolar disorder. They gave me all three together. It was easier to medicate me than to find out what was really the basis for my behavior. They just assumed I had mental health issues. To the system, I was a crazy crackhead. But I was controllable with the drugs. The only problem was the drugs reduced me to a zombie. I couldn't walk. I couldn't function. I'd crawl down the hall of the detention center.

This led to them putting me on suicide watch. I'd be placed in a cell with nothing but a mattress. I was left alone. No one approached me. No one tried to help me. After a while, the separation became real. I longed for some human contact. Even if they didn't care for me, I needed not to be alone. Some of the officers figured this out, and I became an amusement for them. Some of them would flash their lights into my cell and demand that I lay down and spread my legs. I don't know if it was the same officers or other ones who would offer me a piece of gum if I'd give them a blow job. I couldn't say no, so they'd slide their penis through the slot, and I'd perform for them. It was better than nothing, and no one cared.

When I was released, I went back to the streets because the streets were all I knew. The streets were all I could depend on. As insane as it may sound, the streets were home. I was back on the same streets, doing the same thing. I went back underneath the bridge where I felt safe. But the same streets that harbored me were also my worst enemy.

One day while visiting Barbara, my sister and I were standing outside. A van pulled up with two guys from the neighborhood. They asked me what I was doing and if I wanted to get high. They gave me some money to purchase some crack. I took the money and disappeared. I did buy the crack, but I smoked it. Several hours later, I'd forgotten about the incident. I was out on the streets trying to make a quick score when this van pulled up and the driver asked if I wanted to have some fun. I said, "Yeah." I figured a quick trick, and I'd have some money. He drove to a wooded area. We got out of the van and walked to a secluded area. I wasn't too alarmed even when he asked me if I remembered him. I said, "Naw." I didn't remember him.

He shoved me to the ground and began punching me. "Well, I remember you, bitch!" He was one of the two guys from earlier in the day. "You done fucked with the wrong nigger." He kept beating me. Then he snatched up my dress and pushed himself inside me. "Ah paid for dis." I was scared. He never stopped beating me even as he had sex with me. He started to choke me, and I started to black out. Then something said, "Open your eyes!" When I opened my eyes, he'd picked up a big boulder and was holding it above his head. He was about to smash my head in with that rock. I looked up at him, and all I could scream was one name: "Jesus!"

He stopped in midair, as if I'd hit him. He threw the boulder down and stood up. He picked me up and helped me back to the van. Neither of us said anything as he drove me back. I couldn't figure out what had happened. I didn't know why I'd called out that name. I hadn't said that name in a long time. Had Jesus heard me? Had he sent angels to protect me? Did he care about me? After driving me back to the neighborhood where he'd picked me up, this guy gave me his watch because he said he didn't have any money. I remember getting out of his van. I was as surprised and shocked about what had happened as he was. I didn't know Jesus, but He'd saved my life.

He'd saved my life, and I went back to the streets. I didn't stop doing what I'd been doing all along. I kept doing drugs. I kept prostituting. One day, out of desperation, I snatched a woman's purse and ran. By this time, everyone, including the neighborhood policemen, all knew me. I guess when the lady described me, it didn't take Big Black, a local cop, long to find me. "Come on, Tonier. Let's go." After only three months on the streets, I was headed back to jail. And while it hadn't been confirmed by a doctor, I was certain I was pregnant again.

I was back in jail where the medical staff prescribed more psychotropic drugs. I told the nurses I thought I was pregnant, but they said it was a urinary tract infection. The doctor prescribed antibiotics and painkillers. I hurt. I knew something was happening. I begged to be taken off the medication, but they wrote me up as being defiant. So they kept giving me the meds.

One morning, I woke up in pain so bad I could hardly stand. I felt like I needed to have a bowel movement, so I sat down on the commode. I pushed, but when I looked down, the toilet was filled with blood. I screamed. The baby had crowned, and I could see the head of the baby coming out of me. Officers ran into my cell. For a few minutes it was a panic scene as they ran around trying to figure out what to do. Finally, a nurse came down. By this time, I was lying on the floor. She looked at the baby's head sticking out and placed a sheet across my body from the waist down. The other officers handcuffed me to the gurney to make sure I didn't try to escape. I wondered where they thought I was going with a baby hanging out of me.

I was transported to the local hospital where I lay in a hallway on that gurney for three hours. The officers who accompanied me were helpless to help me, and the hospital staff didn't pay me any attention. So I just laid there in pain. At the point when the guards were changing, a doctor finally came over to help me. By that time, the baby was dead, but I still had to go through with the delivery. After all I'd been through, the ER doctor told the guards I should be admitted. When the guards called the supervisor, he told them to bring me back to the center because he didn't have personnel to babysit me. I didn't care. My baby had just died. At that moment, I felt like what they thought I was: nothing. No one ever told me whether the baby was a boy or a girl. Once again, I found myself at a familiar place with a familiar memory, and I found myself reliving the experience at the abortion clinic.

CHAPTER 7

Trapped

I did them no wrong,
but they laid a trap for me.
I did them no wrong, but they
dug a pit to catch me.

—Psalm 35:7

W hen I got back to jail, I went into that black place. I didn't want to die. I just didn't want to exist anymore. I wouldn't eat. I wouldn't shower. I wouldn't talk. I couldn't sleep. I remember thinking, *If I just don't move, they won't see me, and I will stop being.* I'd just sit in my cell. I kept thinking, *I am fading away. One day they won't be able to see me.* I looked into the darkness, and I kept looking. I was so lost I didn't pay attention to what was happening to me physically.

Two days after I'd given birth, I stood up, and the world swirled. I fainted and had to be taken back to the hospital. I don't know if I fainted because I was weak from not eating, or because I was still bleeding so heavily. At the hospital, the doctor decided to do a D and C to remove all the old blood and any remaining tissue. After they scraped my womb, I went back to the detention center, back to the same cell, and back to the blackness that was closing in on me.

I was hollow inside. I felt like there was nothing. Sometimes I'd lie on my stomach to see if I could feel my heart beating. When I could sleep, I had these weird dreams. Sometimes I'd dream about Mil. I'd see her and the baby I'd aborted and the baby who'd been born dead. They'd be with Mil, and she'd be cooking pork chops for them. They looked and sounded so happy. What was strange was that I could never tell if they were boys or girls. Other times, I'd dream about Lil Keith. He'd be running down this long hallway, and I'd be running after him. Then he'd turn a corner, and I could hear him. When I'd get to the corner, he'd be gone and Keith Sr. would be standing there laughing as I begged him to tell me where Lil Keith was. I'd wake up from these dreams sweating and crying.

Another dream that I had often was about that guy who tried to kill me. But instead of him raping me, he'd be chasing me through those woods. Then he'd catch me, and, when he caught me, he'd start beating me. Instead of picking up a rock to smash in my head, he'd start choking me. I could hear myself gasping for air. Then just as I was about to black out, I'd scream "Jesus!" And in my dream, as soon as I said "Jesus," I'd be in this big room filled with light. I didn't see Jesus, but I could feel his presence. It was a clean room with white furniture. No one would be in the room but me, and it seemed like I was waiting for somebody. It felt so good in that room. Usually when I had this dream, I'd wake myself up crying. It always seemed so real.

Visiting rules at the detention center were strictly enforced. People could only receive visitors in the recreation room, so I was surprised when I was laying curled up on my bed one day and a correctional officer (CO) came to my cell. "Cain. You got a visitor." I didn't even move. I figured it was one of the medical staff. I was so surprised when Kathy's red head peeked in.

"Hey, Tonier. How are you?" She always made me feel so safe. I wanted to tell her about all the awful things that had happened to me, but I didn't. I wanted to tell her all about it. I wanted to tell her I was coming apart inside. I was falling into that black hole, and I couldn't stop. I didn't want to stop. No one cared about me or my children. I was totally alone in the world. That is what I wanted to tell Kathy. Instead, I said, "I'm fine," which was a lie.

We visited for more than an hour. Kathy told me she wanted to help me. I wondered why. No one else had wanted to help. Even those people who were supposed to help me, like the drug counselor at the aftercare program who'd raped me, didn't care. Kathy was so different. She didn't seem to be put off by how I looked and smelled. Before she left, she took my hands into hers and said, "Let's pray." I didn't have the strength to tell her that God didn't know me, and I didn't think he cared about me. I just bowed my head and listened to the words she said. "Father, I ask you to bless Tonier and watch over her. Please grant her your richest blessings. I ask this in the name of Jesus. Amen." After she finished praying, she gave me a hug and promised she'd be back.

She did come back, and at the end of each visit, she always prayed and hugged me. I don't know what it was, but I started to look for her and hoped she'd visit. I liked it when she prayed for me. While I didn't know much about praying, I always felt so peaceful after her prayers. I found out much later that one of the COs had contacted Kathy and told her about how sick I was. She'd come to rescue me, and she had. On one of her visits, she informed me that she'd be accompanying me to my next court appearance. She told me she was making arrangements for me to become a part of a Christian program called Teen Challenge. She was excited about the program, so I became excited. But I was afraid that another judge would just commit me to a longer term in prison.

When I went to court, Kathy was there as she'd promised. She'd even brought her husband, Kenneth. They both stood up and asked the judge to release me to them. They explained to the judge that they'd become my sponsors for the Teen Challenge program. I remember looking at the judge sitting there, listening to Kathy and Kenneth and acting like he was genuinely impressed, until he turned to look at me. Then he said, "Tonier. You're being given a real opportunity to change. You know this isn't the first time you've been in my court. Something in me says these good people are wasting their time and money. Something else in me wants to believe you can change." I just looked at him. I didn't cry. I just held my head down as I looked at the floor.

"Look up, so I can see your eyes." I held up my head and looked at the judge and all the other people in the court-room. Everyone was looking at me. "Do you understand what these people are doing for you?" I managed to mumble "yes." "Okay, Mr. and Mrs. Kenney, I want to believe in what you are presenting to this court. Having said that, I am going to release Tonier to your custody. I am going to order that she participate in the Teen Challenge program in Columbus, Ohio. I am instructing my clerk to complete the necessary paperwork so you can be released tonight." With that, I became the ward of Kathy and Kenneth Kenney. I don't know if I can describe how I felt. For the first time in a long time, I cried happy tears.

By seven o'clock that evening, I was at Kathy and Kenneth's house. They'd made arrangements for me to stay in their daughter's bedroom. Kathy had purchased clothing for me from the church's thrift store. For the first time in a long time, I took a shower. There were no prying eyes watching me as I bathed. It was wonderful. The smell of that pink bath soap was divine. I let the warm water run down my body. Kathy's daughter's room had a waterbed. That night for the first time in a long time, I slept. I fell asleep, and I slept. I wasn't bothered by the dreams. Sleeping at Kathy's house was so peaceful, and I felt so safe.

I stayed with Kathy and Kenneth for a few days before I left for Columbus. In those few days, I was treated like a daughter. Both Kathy and Kenneth were so kind to me. If they had been black, I could've been their daughter. That's how they treated me. I actually started trying to pray because the two of them were praying for me. On the night before I was supposed to leave for Columbus, Kathy gave me a going-away party. No one had ever given me a party. I was so excited. Kathy had invited some of the ladies from her church, and they bought me little gifts to take with me. I was so happy. This felt even better than being back at Mil's house. The only thing missing were those mouthwatering pork chops!

The next morning after the party, Kathy took me to the airport. I was scared and happy and nervous. It was the first time I'd been on an airplane, and it was the first time I'd been this far from Annapolis. I was very nervous, but I was excited about going to Teen Challenge. I really wanted to make Kathy proud. She'd been so good to me. She believed in me.

I didn't know what to expect in Columbus, but I was happy to be going. Teen Challenge is a Christian-based program that helps women overcome life-controlling addictions. It was a residential drug and alcohol rehabilitation program that was in a big house about five blocks from the Ohio State University football stadium. Unfortunately, it sat between two fraternity houses, and, on football weekends when the Buckeyes were playing, the drunk fraternity boys marched around the house chanting MC Hammer's song "Pray."

No one had prepared me for the biggest challenge: home-sickness. It came in waves like the withdrawal from drugs. I missed Kathy and Kenneth. I missed the streets. I even missed the detention center. But I found a group of young women just like me who were trying to crawl out of some kind of self-destructive behavior. We quickly formed new friendships that made being away from home a little less stressful. All of the other girls had experienced some of what I'd experienced. We had that in common. Some of us had come from the streets; others were from more privileged homes. One new friend I made was a girl named Tammy from upstate New York. Tammy had been sent to Teen Challenge by her parents. Although we were complete opposites, we became good friends.

Our daily routine started with prayer and then we'd spend time reading the Bible. After Bible study, we each had chores in the house. I liked it at Teen Challenge, but it didn't really help me get better. We read the Bible and we prayed, but no one really explained how to develop a personal relationship with God. I'd experienced the power of the name of Jesus, but I wondered how I'd done that. I had a lot of questions that no one answered. I also thought it was strange that we didn't receive any kind of counseling or therapy. So most of the time after Bible study, prayers, and chores, we'd sit around and reminisce about our lives back home and getting high. In fact, we spent most of our free time talking about how we missed getting high.

When Thanksgiving came, most of the girls went home. I spent Thanksgiving with a Mexican family from Toledo, Ohio. They came down and picked me up. We spent Thanksgiving with some friends of theirs. It was different. For Thanksgiving dinner we had a traditional turkey with all the fixings, but we also had some of their Spanish dishes. They seemed like good people who really wanted me to do well. They were a Christian family, and they prayed for me. Everyone was praying for me.

Everyone talked about Jesus. While I knew His name, and I had witnessed His power, I didn't really know Him.

The time between Thanksgiving and Christmas seemed to fly by. Kathy and Kenny flew me home for Christmas. It felt different flying back into Annapolis. When the plane arrived, there was Kathy, her red head bobbing above the crowd. She hugged me, and I really felt like she was glad I was home. As we drove back to Arnold, Maryland, which is where Kathy lived, we had time to talk about Teen Challenge. She told me how proud she was of me. I didn't tell her about the longing for drugs or the lies that I'd told the other girls. I wanted Kathy to be proud of me. Aside from Mil and Ann, she was the only other person who'd made me feel secure and safe, and I needed both.

When I got back to her and Kenny's house, the house was beautifully decorated. There was a Christmas tree with presents. It reminded me of being at Ann's house that first Christmas after being taken away from Barbara. There was the same excitement in the air. Kenny and Kathy made me feel like their daughter. They showered me with gifts and love. I didn't have any money, so I wrote them a poem.

Friendship Beyond Kindness

THIS POEM IS DEDICATED TO TWO VERY SPECIAL PEOPLE,
KATHY AND KENNETH KENNEY

You started to care for me, when I was down and wouldn't see
My heart was so worn down
I often wondered how this could be!

Though my pain became more intensified,
I found it hard to even cry
I didn't know how I was going to get by,
or if I could walk my next mile.

Then in my darkness hour,
your friendship started
like a beautiful flower!

Your love was so overwhelming, precious, and rare;
Now my days are filled with happiness,
and I know how much you care!

I can't begin to say "Thank you" for all you've done for me.
I guess I should say, "Thanks be to God!"
What wonderful people He made you to be.
Our Lord and Savior has blessed me greatly,
with your friendship and your love:
The Lord has cared for me as if I were a gentle dove.

Oh God, thank you for Kathy and Kenneth,
Their friendship is like a warm touch;
They alone have given me so much!

I remember when my life was filled with sadness,
and I thought there was no hope;
But Kathy and Kenneth have given me
"friendship beyond kindness,"
and with that and God, I can cope!

I love you both!

On Christmas day, Kathy took me over to Peter Rabbit's house to see Terance and Teli. Although he and Carol were divorced, Peter Rabbit was still taking care of my brother and sister. We had a great afternoon together just sitting around talking and listening to Peter Rabbit's records.

I didn't realize how much I missed Annapolis until I went back to Columbus. Then everything and everyone got on my nerves. The regular Bible reading, the praying to a God who I didn't think cared about me, the silly little girls who knew nothing about really being grown-up, all irritated me. "Huh! Y'all don't know nothin' about a good time. Till you know the love of a good man, don't talk to me about being a woman." Then I told them stories about my boyfriend, who was a big-time drug dealer in Annapolis. Of course, I lied. I exaggerated about the good times. I told them that my "man" would give us anything we wanted. I didn't tell them about living under a bridge. I didn't mention the rapes or the beatings. I didn't tell them that the state had taken my children away from me because I was unfit to be a mother. I didn't tell them about being hungry or going unwashed. I didn't tell them about going to jail, being deloused, or being in a place so black that I didn't think I could get out. I didn't tell them that. I told them about the thrill of getting high. We talked about the feeling of escaping. It sounded so good. I convinced myself. After a week or so of this talk, I decided I was tired of Teen Challenge and I was going home.

I went to the office and told the leaders I wanted to go home. They called Kathy, but she wasn't at home. Since this was before cell phones, they couldn't reach her. And I wasn't going to hang around until she came because I knew she'd talk me out of leaving. I demanded the money Kathy and Kenny had left for bus fare when I entered the program. My friend, Tammy, decided she wanted to go with me, so the two of us went to the bus station. Before the bus left for Annapolis, however, we got drunk. Then we boarded the bus and headed back to my failures.

When we got to Annapolis, I took Tammy to Bridget's apartment. I didn't have to explain to Tammy that there was no boyfriend. I think she knew. We slept on the floor at Bridget's because we didn't have a choice. I went back to earning a living the only way I knew how, and I introduced my little friend from upstate New York to the world of prostitution. At first, she was nervous, but we needed money to purchase drugs and to eat, and prostitution provided both. Sometimes, we'd work together as a team. But this didn't last long. When Tammy's parents found out where she was, they came and took her home.

I didn't stay with Bridget long. The streets continued to call me. I found security in the dangers in the streets. I went back to the bridge where I'd lived with Earl. I wandered the streets looking for that next high. I lied, cheated, and stole to survive. I went back to the section of town where Barbara had lived in the Allen Apartments to prostitute. Bailey was gone. The drug dealer was gone. None of the old neighborhood people were still around. I was surprised to find that the area that had been predominantly black was now mostly Mexican. It didn't matter. While they didn't always speak English, they knew how to purchase sex, so I still had a fairly consistent clientele. They also used drugs, so I had a source.

Life didn't mean anything to me. I'd lost children. I saw Barbara every now and then. Everyone who'd loved or cared about me didn't really seem interested in what I was doing or where I was going. I still didn't sleep well. When I did sleep, I was haunted by dreams of Lil Keith being taken, or Brandon calling me as men pulled him away, or Whitney crying as some unknown woman held her and sang to her. When I wasn't high, I remembered the pain of giving birth to one dead baby and aborting another, both at five months. I remembered. The drugs only allowed me to forget while I was high, so I tried to stay high.

Then one day I was out on the street trying to earn some money when I got busted by a vice policeman. I knew he was an officer when I walked up to the car, but my need to get money to buy drugs outweighed the danger. "You wanna have some fun?" I asked when the car pulled over.

"How much, Brown Sugar?"

"Pends on what you want." I was so desperate. I didn't even ask if he was a police, which is what you do when you're out on the street.

"Round the world."

"Twenty dollars."

"Meet you around the corner."

I knew when I walked away from him that it was a setup, but I needed that twenty dollars. I needed to buy. I needed to escape. When I turned the corner, I was so whacked-out and desperate that I walked into the alley and waited. The car pulled into the alley and stopped. He got out and asked me again about the cost. The next thing I knew I was being placed in handcuffs and put in the back of a bus. At police headquarters, they found out I had an outstanding warrant for parole violation. Since Teen Challenge was a court-ordered program, by leaving, I'd violated my parole.

CHAPTER 8

Shattered Hope

The Lord is my inheritance;
therefore, I will hope in him!

—Lamentations 3:24

I was back in jail, and I was pregnant again with my sixth child. The court ordered that I be sent to the Center for Addiction and Pregnancy (CAP), a program for pregnant inmates at Francis Scott Key Hospital. Being in that hospital where Whitney was born brought back painful memories. There I was again. Why didn't someone ask what was happening to me? Why didn't someone notice the cycle? They didn't. If they did, no one said anything. Instead, my parole officer told me I had to find some place to go since the program at the hospital only allowed me to stay until the baby was born.

My third son, Joshua, was born on December 31, 1991, and we went to the Chrysalis House to live. The Chrysalis House was a program for substance-addicted pregnant and parenting women. The counselors there connected patients to programs that improved their lives. After some research I found out that I only needed one credit to complete high school. I'd always wanted to finish school. So at age twenty-five, I went back to night school. It was so different. I'd study with Joshua on my lap. I'd read as I rocked him to sleep. It looked like I was finally getting back to a normal life. I was excited, but I knew that there was still a dark side to my life. All my hard work finally paid off, and June 1, 1992, I graduated with a high school diploma.

I graduated one night and started college the very next day. On June 2, 1992, I started Anne Arundel Community College as a work-study student. Life was really great. I was starting to live the American dream. I'd messed up, but I'd cleaned myself up. I'd fallen down, but I'd gotten up. I was being a good mother. I had my son with me. I was taking remedial classes in preparation for enrolling in collegiate classes in August. I was actually excited. I wanted to call Kathy and tell her about how well I was doing, but I didn't. I was still so unsure of myself. I made it through my first semester.

Joshua was now almost eight months old. He was pulling himself up and trying to walk. He was a joy. When I looked at him, I saw all my other children, and another chance for me to be a good mother. We were still living in the Chrysalis House. It was August, and I'd gotten a Pell Grant that allowed me to register for a full course load. I was really excited, but Whitney's birthday was August 13, and I remembered.

One afternoon, I was called into a meeting with the administrator of the Chrysalis House. I was informed I'd been released. I couldn't understand why. They told me it was because I'd come in after curfew. I couldn't understand. I was earning As and Bs in college. Joshua was doing well. I acted offended and outraged. But I knew why. The administrator looked genuinely disappointed when she informed me that I'd lied about coming in late. She sounded like that judge who'd said, "You are no better than a rapist!" To me, she seemed to be saying I'd never amount to anything.

There I was again, out on the street with a little baby. I had no place to go and no one to turn to. I remembered my god-mother, Alice White, whom we called Suzanne. I took Joshua to her and asked her to please keep him until I could get back up on my feet. Suzanne had diabetes really bad, but she allowed me and my baby to move in with her and her boyfriend. When she asked me about why I'd been put out of the program, I lied to her and said I didn't know. I knew. Although I said I was clean, I was using. That's the real reason I was released from the Chrysalis House. Somehow they'd found out that I lied.

At this point in my life, I lost all hope and control. I needed money, so I stole from Suzanne. I was too ashamed to go back to her house, so I just left Joshua because I knew she'd take care of him. And I went back to the streets. This time I went back with twenty-eight years of guilt, shame, and hurt. I tried all possible ways I could to kill myself. I drank as much as pos-sible. I used drugs. I abused my body. I did it all to the extreme. There were no Mils or Anns or Kathys to pull me back. No Mils or Anns or Kathys to make me feel safe or cared about. There was no one.

One evening I was out on the corner trying to pick up some money when a car pulled up. I didn't recognize it, but the driver called me by name. "Hey, Neen." When I looked in the car, I don't know who I was expecting to see, but I was shocked to see Keith Cain. I jumped back and started to walk away. He called me again. "Hey, Neen." Something in me said Run, don't walk! But the drugs were talking louder than anything else, so I stopped and turned around.

"Git in." It was strange, but with Keith I became that old Tonier who didn't say anything. I got in and just sat in the corner of his truck looking at him. I was street dirty. I couldn't imagine why he'd even acknowledge that he knew me. "So dis what you done come to? I heard you were working down here. What happened to you?" What happened to me? When he said that, something inside me snapped. I sat up and pure hate came out of me. I wanted to say, "You stole my child. You ripped out my heart and threw it against the wall. You killed any hope of living I had." That's what I wanted to say.

Instead, I said, "Where Lil Keith?" Then I started to cry. I started begging Keith to tell me where my son was. I hadn't seen him in years. I wanted to know if he was still alive. I wanted to know how he looked. I wanted to know who he was calling mama. I wanted to know about my child. And all Keith did was sit there looking at me. Then he pulled out a picture. It was Lil Keith. He was so beautiful. I really started to cry and plead with Keith to give me the picture.

"Tell you what. You do something for me, and I'll give you this picture." I would've done anything for that picture. And I did. I gave Keith oral sex. When I climbed out of his truck, I just stood in the street and looked at that picture. Lil Keith had grown into a beautiful little boy. He was smiling. He looked so happy. My heart ached. I tried to reach into that picture to touch my child. My child! My soul cried for him. Then the drugs said, *Come on, Neen. We got your back.* So I went back to this crack house where I was sleeping, and my friend had some rocks that she shared with me.

Every so often Keith showed up and wanted me to service him. After that first night when he demanded oral sex for the picture of our son, I always charged him. Somewhere in my drugged-out mind, I realized Keith had taken advantage of me, and I wasn't going to let that happen again.

One day my sister Teli found me. She told me that Suzanne was now completely blind from diabetes. I'd almost forgotten Joshua. I hadn't been to see him in a while. My whole life was about pain and the drugs I used to ease the pain. I learned from Teli that Suzanne's boyfriend had physically abused Joshua, so I wrote a letter to the Department of Social Services and asked that custody of my son be given to my sister. Teli was able to get Joshua. She was not able to keep him, however. He was eventually placed in foster care and adopted. By the time he was placed in foster care, I was back in jail.

By now my life was a cycle of living on the streets, committing crimes, and going to jail or prison. No one now attempted to save me from myself. No judges ordered court-mandated programs. They realized I was a waste of time and money. I was a failure, and even the system knew it. I lived in a world of shame. I was a failure. I was a disappointment to everyone, including myself. I was very thin from all the drug use and not eating.

All I wanted was to forget all the hurt. I needed to forget the lost children. I needed to forget the lost innocence. I needed to forget the broken marriage. I needed to forget how and what people had done to me. I had to forget all the things that had been said about me and to me. I had to forget. But I couldn't forget, and, despite all the drugs I used, the memories stayed with me. Despite my desire to die, I was still breathing. I'd reached the lowest place in my life, and I couldn't stop.

CHAPTER 9

Healing Neen

Therefore if any man be in Christ,
he is a new creature: old things are
passed away; behold, all things
are become new.

—2 Corinthians 5:17 (KJV)

Then something miraculous happened. I was born on March 15, 2004, when I was thirty-seven years old. It's not the day I was born into this world, but it was the day that I was born again and became the person I am today. There is a story in the New Testament where Jesus says to Nicodemus, "You must be born again." Then Nicodemus asks the question, "How can a man be born when he is old? Can he enter the second time into his mother's womb?" (John 3:4). Good question. I was born again that day and became a new person.

Prior to that date, I went through a lot of terrible and life-altering experiences. But what made that day so significant was that I came to fully know and accept the fact that there is a benevolent God who loves me, who hears me when I pray, and who answers my prayers. That's right—He loves *me*. *He* loves me. He *loves* me. He had always loved me. He'd always been there watching over me and protecting me. Suddenly, the children's song "Jesus Loves Me" became real.

Jesus loves Tonier. Jesus *loved* Tonier Cain. All I ever wanted was for somebody to love me, someone to say, "Tonier, I love you. I will always love you." It sounds rather simple, but it was a big deal in my broken life. Like a lot of people, I'd sought love and acceptance in all the wrong places: drugs, alcohol, men, and sex. They lasted for a minute, but they were temporary. And I always came away feeling cheap and dirty. I know because I'd tried them all in *big* ways. One thing about me is that I never halfheartedly did anything.

Prior to that cold day in March, I'd done some pretty sinful things. I'd been a prostitute, a drug addict, a thief, and an alcoholic. You name it, and I'd probably tried it at least once and sometimes twice. I'd been beaten, raped, gone to jail, had six babies, been married, been through rehab, and flunked out of rehab. But I was still hollow inside. There was something missing.

I was pregnant again and running from the law. I was hiding out at my unborn baby's father's house where I'd been bingeing on alcohol for days. There was a knock at the door and a man asked for me. I went to the door. He was a normal-looking guy, nothing special. I couldn't place him, but he asked for me.

"Are you Tonier Cain?"

"Yeah."

"Put your hands up. You are under arrest." With that, my world stood still. He pulled a gun and pointed it directly at my face. I was scared. He was a bounty hunter who'd come to find me.

I was rearrested and ended up back in prison. I was terrified at the thought of losing another child. Suddenly, the memory of losing my kids kept coming back. My husband had taken

Lil Keith and hidden him. I'd aborted a baby. Brandon and Whitney were both snatched by the police and a social worker. I could still hear Brandon screaming, "Mommie! Mommie!" Then there was the stillborn child and Joshua, who was taken into foster care. One, two, three, four, five, six—all gone. Forever gone out of my life. There was no chance of me ever getting them back. I could imagine them calling some other woman "Mommie." I thought about them learning to walk and running into someone else's arms. I tortured myself thinking how someone else had replaced me as their Mommie. Someone else dried their tears. Someone else protected them; someone else loved them; someone else cared for them. It wasn't right. I was supposed to be their mother. I was supposed to be there like Barbara was never there for me. I couldn't let them take this baby away.

I actually was making myself sick by worrying about what would go wrong this time. I needed something to break right for me. I found myself wondering about Kathy. I had always felt safe with her, but I'd lost contact. And I didn't want to jinx her life. I had to do something. About this time someone told me about a program that was being offered. It was called T.A.M.A.R's Children. "T.A.M.A.R" was an acronym for Trauma, Addiction, Mental Health, and Recovery. The name came from the biblical story of King David's daughter, Tamar, who had been raped by her half-brother. This program was different from other programs because it addressed the trauma women had experienced. That was new to me. I'd been to well-meaning prison psychologists and addiction counselors, but no one had ever addressed the things that had happened to me and my inability to deal, let alone cope, with those things. T.A.M.A.R's Children did. This program would also allow me to keep this baby. Hallelujah! More than any other thing in the whole world, I wanted to keep this baby.

I'd decided to name her Orlandra. And I'd promised myself to make up for all the mistakes that had taken my other children away. I was going to care for this baby. I was going to love her. I was going to protect her. She was going to love me. I'd be hers, and she'd be mine.

The staff from T.A.M.A.R's Children told me I was a perfect candidate. But nothing had ever come easy in my life, and this was no exception. The warden at the prison where I was serving time wouldn't allow me to participate in the program because I had to be eligible for parole, and I was in jail for violation of parole—another roadblock—but I was determined. From somewhere in my past, I remembered somebody saying to me, "If all else fails, look up and ask God." Why not? I'd tried other things and none of them worked.

I lay on the floor of my prison cell curled in a fetal position, and I prayed. I prayed like my ancestors prayed for deliverance. I prayed a prayer of desperation. I prayed from the bottom of my heart. I prayed in earnest. I didn't know the form or format for "real" prayer, but I prayed out of my soul. Years later, I think

I must have prayed like Hannah when she asked God to give her a child.

"God, if You are listening, this is Tonier. I have done a lot of bad things. You know the things I have done, but You are the only one who can change this situation, and You are the only one who can change me. And I want to change. I don't want to lose my baby. Please help me. If it's Your will for me to take care of her, I need You to make this happen. Please. I need You to provide, so I can take care of her. If it's not Your will, I don't want to hurt her. I don't want her to go through anything I've been through. If You allow me to keep her, I'll give her back to You."

I prayed. I cried out to God. At that time I didn't know that the Bible says, "The effectual fervent prayer of a righteous man availeth much" (James 5:16, KJV). I didn't know that. I just knew that God was the only one who could turn this situation around. That morning I prayed with the fervor of a desperate woman because I had nothing to lose, and, if God heard me, I'd gain what I wanted most—my daughter. I now understood the verse in the Bible about Jesus praying "fervently, and he was in such agony of spirit that His sweat fell to the ground like great drops of blood" (Luke 22:44). I prayed that morning with every fiber in my body. I was honest with God, which was something I'd never been with anyone else, including myself.

I prayed that morning in a cell in the Maryland Institute for Women-Jessup. I went boldly to the throne of grace with my petition. I didn't know if God had time for me or even wanted me. Nobody else had. Everybody had left; everyone I'd cared about was either gone or didn't really care. Mil died and left me; Barbara never seemed to want me around. Keith had left. All the many nameless men were gone. Even my children were gone. If God didn't hear me, I'd understand, but I was hoping He'd answer my prayer.

I don't know how long I prayed. I just remember that when I got up off the floor I felt relieved. To this day I can't explain the relieved sensation. If I had to describe it, it would be like having on a heavy coat, and then, when you take the coat off, even though it's been warm, you realize how heavy that coat was. Looking back on that time, I now know that I had released all my cares into God's hands. I'd actually put myself and my unborn child in His hands for safekeeping. I knew in my heart that if He'd heard me, I'd do all in my power to live up to my promise.

This was when the new Tonier Cain was born. When I got up off that floor, I knew that something about me had changed. It wasn't the way I walked or looked. It was something else. I couldn't explain it then. Looking back, I now know that it was because finally, after all those years, I'd found a safe place. I'd found what was always there. I just didn't have the willpower to believe it could exist in my ragged life because no one else had shown me love.

The therapist from T.A.M.A.R's Children went back to the warden and pleaded my case. I don't know what she said, but whatever she said touched the warden's heart and eventually persuaded her that I was willing to spend more time in jail in order to go to this program. She agreed. I went back to the court and asked for additional time, and they granted my request. Then I was accepted into the program.

Prayer works! God had heard my heart's cry. He had mercy on me. I felt His love. I realized that, in the midst of all my mess, God really did care about me. He was watching over me. It was as if a veil was peeled back, and, for the first time in my entire life, I felt true, unconditional love. I knew without a doubt that God loved me.

When I was released from prison, I went directly to T.A.M.A.R's Children. It was like nothing I'd ever seen. The woman who greeted me at the door had a huge smile. "You must be Tonier. I am so glad you have come. Come on in." She was glad I was there? That was a new one. No one had been glad for me to be anywhere, except gone. She seemed really sincere, and I felt at ease. After nineteen years of living on the streets, and anywhere else I could find a place to lay my head, someone was actually glad to see me. Her presence and reaction to me offered me hope and said that this could be the beginning I'd prayed for—a new beginning for a new me. God was actually outdoing Himself. He'd given me a new place and transformed me into a new person. That wasn't too bad. There was a calmness about this place. I liked it.

I was given my own room with a crib and bassinette. I was so happy. I had a safe place for me and my baby. For all I cared, I could've been at the best hotel in the world. I even had a refrigerator in my room! This really was a new beginning. What I wasn't expecting was what happened next.

Soon after getting settled into my new place, I met with my trauma therapist. That's when I began to face the monsters in my life. One of the first things I learned was that "trauma" was the name of those personal "things" that had happened to me. That was a new one on me! Before this, other counselors and psychologists had told me I had substance-abuse problems or that I was bipolar or schizophrenic. Some of these things were true; I knew I had some of these problems. But at the mental health wards, they told me I was crazy and kept giving me medication, which made me crazier. None of this had worked.

My trauma therapist told me, "Everything that happened to you as a child, you didn't do to yourself." That was new to me. I'd always blamed myself for all my problems. If I'd been pretty enough, Barbara might have loved me. If I'd been strong enough, those men may not have taken advantage of me. If I'd been a better person, Mil may not have died. If I'd been a good mother, Keith wouldn't have taken Lil Keith and I'd still have Brandon, Whitney, and Joshua. If I'd been a better wife, I'd still be married, if not to Keith then to Mike. If, if, if.

In all my life, no one had ever asked me about what had happened to me when I was a child or why I used drugs. Not one counselor or psychologist had ever asked. Not one teacher had ever asked. Ann and her daughters had never asked. It had taken me all those years to finally come to a place, with God's help, where someone realized that something had happened to me all those years ago, someone who realized I hadn't just woke up one morning and decided to be a drug addict and a prostitute. She said, "Tell me about it." And I began to tell her about what had happened to me as a child.

It was good to be able to finally get those things out, but it was hard. I cried and cried. As I told her about years of broken dreams and lost innocence, I cried and cried some more. I didn't know it then, but crying is good. I cried about all the beatings that Barbara had given me. I cried about the times that drunken men had forced themselves on an innocent nine-year-old child. I cried about the times that Barbara had ignored our needs. I cried for the nights that my brothers and sisters and I had gone hungry. I cried because all I ever wanted was for my mother to say she loved me, and she never did. I cried for the times I'd heard Oatmeal abuse Barbara. I cried cleansing tears as all the hurt of what people had done to me came out. I cried healing tears as I began to realize it wasn't my fault. I was actually a victim of other people's actions.

I'd built a wall around my feelings. Never once had I cried as a child when those nameless men had forced themselves upon me. I never cried out for help, not once. So many years of pain. So much guilt. So much hurt. I cried as I faced the demons in my life. My therapist and I dealt with all the neglect and the abandonment. I cried some more. There were times when I was in therapy sessions that I'd cry so much, we couldn't even finish the sessions. There were times when I'd just rock back and forth as I cried, and my therapist would rock with me.

I cried in those therapy sessions, but I also cried out in my heart. *Oh, God! This is too painful. God, please. I know You hear me. Please. Give me the strength.* And I kept on crying and kept on talking. I started to learn that I was not responsible for Barbara being how she was. It was not my fault. I learned that I had to release her because I couldn't carry her any longer. I couldn't take on her character or babysit her life by my attempts to provide for her to make her love me. I couldn't, and the Lord knows I'd tried. I learned I had to love myself and respect myself in order to receive love and respect.

My counselor assured me I was doing fine. I didn't feel fine. I was emotionally tired. I was drained. But I knew I had to keep going. Finally, I had someone who was actually listening to me, someone who wanted to know what had happened to Tonier. I trusted her. She made me feel safe.

"I can't do this," I told my therapist one day.

"Tonier, you can. Just don't try to do it by yourself. I'm here."

I worked on all my issues, from prostituting to being raped over and over again. I told her about the many beatings from all the different people. I told her about stealing and sleeping underneath bridges or in abandoned houses. I talked and cried, and she listened. I rocked and cried, and she rocked and listened. If I was crying about something, she didn't smile and try to make me think that life was a "bed of roses" or give me a pep talk about how "things will get better." She allowed me to release all my anger and frustrations. She didn't rush me. Never did I see her look at her watch. She was patient.

There were times when I did a lot of repeating, and she never said, "You covered that already." She allowed me to get it *all* out. I needed to get it all out. So much had happened to me I couldn't remember it all. One thing I couldn't talk about was my kids and the abortion and miscarriage. When I got to those experiences, I just couldn't move forward.

"Tonier, you are not alone. I am here," my therapist reassured me. Sometimes I cried so much I had the dry heaves. That's when I had used up all my tears, but I was still crying. From way down inside me, God gave me the strength to keep going. I kept feeling that lightness I'd felt when I'd prayed in that prison cell. I knew God was with me and I was doing the right thing. So I kept talking, and I kept crying.

I learned that many of the choices I'd made in my life were responses to the trauma that had happened to me. The behaviors I'd used to cope with the trauma were like the symptoms of a disease. One of the failings of all the other programs I'd been through was that they only treated the outer behavior, not the deeper issues that had led to it. They tried to put good on top of the shit in my life, and, when you do that, all you have is a pile of shit with whipped cream on top. The problem is, it still smells like shit and it still feels like shit because it is shit.

At T.A.M.A.R's Children I was forced to dig down deep to get out all the nasty, dirty, bad-smelling, foul, funky, rotten, decaying, dead issues and air out those places where they'd lived. Then and only then was I able to replace those issues with positive affirmations. I learned that you've got to get the bad out before you can bring in the good. And you've got to replace the bad with good or the bad will return to haunt you. This was what I learned in dealing with the trauma that had happened in my life. Did it hurt? Yeah! But these layers of pain had to be uncovered and released in order for me to begin to experience true freedom, particularly mental and emotional freedom.

As I continued therapy, I learned that there is truly a huge difference between counseling and therapy. In all those other programs, I was counseled about drugs and their effects, and all that made me was a very informed drug addict. Therapy, however, forced me to face and deal with the issues that had driven me to use drugs. There's a big difference between the two methods. Through T.A.M.A.R's Children I met the *real* Tonier Cain; I learned who she was and what she was capable of doing. Trauma therapy opened the door for me to discover what needed to be done as I moved toward healing Neen.

My healing started with me. I'd hated myself for so long. I hated my weakness. I hated the fact that all my life I'd not had a voice. I hated the fact that, when people pushed, I'd step back. One of the first things I learned in therapy was that I am a good person. I learned that the problem was not with me; it was with the people who took advantage of me. I learned to finally love myself because I did have worth. From my earliest remembrances, I'd been Neen, short for Deneen. Now I became Tonier. I put away old things, and I became a new creature, as the Bible says (2 Corinthians 5:17). When I looked in the mirror, I saw a beautiful, clean, poised woman. I now had a voice. The therapist helped me learn that I could speak up for myself; that I *must* speak up for myself.

As I began to heal, I opened up that place inside where I'd hidden all the pain and hurt. It was full. I learned to bring things out of the darkness because when I confronted them, they disappeared. I took out fear, and I learned in therapy how to confront my fears. I learned all the triggers that brought back my fears. I learned to confront the smell of fear. I took Keith and our marriage out of that dark place. I learned what Keith had done to me was wrong, and possibly illegal. I took the abortion out of that place, and I learned I had to forgive myself because people do make mistakes. I took Barbara out of that place. I learned to love my mother without being responsible for her actions. I took the abuse out of that dark place. I learned it wasn't my fault.

One of the most difficult things I had in that hidden place was the relationship I didn't have with Barbara. I was traumatized by what had and what hadn't happened between me and my mother. The one relationship I'd craved the most was with Barbara. I craved her approval; I sought her love. Most of the trauma had occurred because of her. Facing that problem was extremely difficult. In therapy, I learned to understand what triggered my responses to her. I learned to accept Barbara for who she was. I learned to accept that she was not my responsibility. I learned to love her whether she loved me in return or not. I had to admit that, although I craved her approval, I was a good person without it. I learned to love Barbara. I learned I couldn't continue to protect and shelter Barbara. But I never stopped wanting to. I learned not to make her problems mine. I finally learned that Barbara and everything that had happened to her were God's problem.

Trust was a huge issue in my healing. From the many things that had happened to me, I had learned not to trust anyone. Everyone whom I'd trusted had failed me. I trusted Barbara, and she had failed to protect me. I trusted Ann, and she didn't ask what had happened to me. I trusted Keith, and he stole my heart and my child. My list goes on and on. In therapy, I learned that trust isn't dependency. I learned to stand up for Tonier. I learned that I do have a valid voice, and I have a right to speak up for myself.

My healing included finally becoming a real mother, not just a woman who'd had a baby. The program taught me how to form a natural attachment to my daughter, Orlandra. When she was first born, I wanted to breast-feed, but I was afraid I might be HIV positive. So I took the test and waited. The wait felt like a lifetime. When I found out that I was not HIV positive, I began breast-feeding. Through breast-feeding, I was able to form a natural bond with my daughter. And in breast-feeding, I came to realize how God provides.

At first, I was so protective I could barely stand to be separated from Orlandra. When we had group therapy, a very nice woman named Pat Shea watched the children. I remember telling Miss Pat, "I'm Tonier, Orlandra's mother. If she cries, please call me. And don't let the older children hurt her." I'm sure she stifled a laugh at my directions, but she was very kind and always said the same thing, "She'll be alright." True to her word, Orlandra was fine with Miss Pat. So I learned from Miss Pat that loving didn't mean clinging or smothering. Pat and I eventually became the best of friends, and as a result I made her Orlandra's guardian in case anything should happen to me.

I also learned how to have a relationship with God. After all the years of hearing people talk about God and Jesus, I learned that He does love me. I learned that God loved me so much that He gave His only Son for a former drug-taking, prostituting thief like me. I learned that all those years when I was on the street, He'd been watching over and protecting me, despite my reckless ways. I learned that Ann's prayers and Kathy's prayers had kept me safe even when I didn't know it. I know it had to be God, because when I was tested for HIV, the tests were negative. I also learned that I can have a relationship with Jesus. I learned He is within me, and I came to accept that God loves me in spite of my failings and shortcomings.

CHAPTER 10

Another Chance

So faith comes from hearing,
and hearing by the word of Christ.

—Romans 10:17 (NAS)

I learned. T.A.M.A.R's Children taught me. When I graduated in 2005, Andi Karfgin, one of the founders of the program, offered me a job. I was so happy. Andi told me I was employable, and she trusted me! So she hired me to do a job that I had no idea how to do. And she allowed me to learn how to be an acting case manager. Andi also continued to mentor me. She was Jewish, but she liked to laugh and remind us, "I may be Jewish, but everything I do is Christian." In the new job, I escorted new women to doctor's appointments or social service appointments and waited for the new clients as they attended these appointments. Within three months, I was promoted to Peer Support at the sister program for T.A.M.A.R's Children called T.A.M.A.R's Community for Women. Women in this program were prostitutes with mental health issues. I worked hard to prove to Andi that her trust was not misplaced. As a result of my hard work, I was promoted as Andi's executive assistant at T.A.M.A.R's Children.

With the new position came new responsibilities. I knew that, although I tried to be good, my success was due to the favor of God on my life, a fact I didn't take lightly. Andi saw change in me, and she continued to mentor me and give me additional opportunities. To prove she trusted me, a part of my new duties included handling finances for the corporation. She actually gave me the corporation's checkbook—me, a forger who'd written so many bad checks that a judge had ordered I not even have a crayon in my hands! But Andi said she saw something in me. She saw a new Tonier reformed by the grace of God. She saw a woman moving in the favor of the Lord. And while I couldn't explain it, I was beginning to accept the fact that God's favor ain't fair.

Every day gave me a new opportunity. Every day allowed me another chance to "work out my own salvation in trembling and fear" (Philippians 2:12–13). I was so glad Andi believed in me, encouraged me, guided me, and trusted me. By the time she went home to be with the Lord in 2007, I'd become a stronger and more confident person because of her.

One day prior to Andi's home-going, I told her about Kathy and her husband and how they'd believed in me and had tried to help me. I told her about how I'd been a mess and had messed up the opportunity Kathy had attempted to provide. I was still ashamed of how I'd taken advantage of Kathy and Kenneth's trust. Andi suggested I call Kathy. I was hesitant, but Andi said, "Kathy's a woman of God. Trust her heart." So I mustered up the courage and dialed Kathy.

When the familiar voice answered the phone, I almost hung up. But I said, "Kathy. This is Tonier." I think she started to cry. She kept saying my name over and over. Then I started to cry. I was so glad to hear her voice and that she hadn't hung up.

After a while, she finally said, "Tonier, you don't know how many times I've wondered where you were. I used to check the newspaper expecting to see your obituary." I wanted to tell her there were times when I should've been in the obituaries. But my life was proof that God's "grace is sufficient, and His strength is made perfect in weakness" (2 Corinthians 12:9).

I poured out my heart to Kathy. I told her about everything I could remember since the last time we'd spoken. I told her about Joshua. I told her about sinking to the bottom. I told her about Orlandra and the second chance God had given me through T.A.M.A.R's Children. We talked and talked as I witnessed to her about the faithfulness of God in my life. It felt so good to talk to her. We agreed to meet. As I hung up, I couldn't help but think that much of my success was a result of Kathy and Kenneth's prayers for me. I could close my eyes and still hear her saying, "Keep Tonier, in the name of Jesus." Now I knew that same Jesus! It was a great feeling.

In addition to giving me a job, T.A.M.A.R's Children, unlike other programs, didn't just send me out on my own. It helped me find housing through its Section 8 Shelter and Care grant. My first place was a one-bedroom furnished apartment in Towson, Maryland. It wasn't grand, but it was home, the first home I'd had in a long time. T.A.M.A.R's Children sent someone to help me with the basics of living on my own and keeping a house. I was also provided with a case manager who helped me develop a budget and taught me money management.

Life was not without challenges. There were days when I was afraid. Then I'd read 2 Timothy 1:7: "For God has not given us a spirit of fear and timidity, but of power, love, and self-discipline." I'd remember I was not alone. When I wasn't feeling too brave, I'd just repeat that verse over and over again. After a while, I'd start to feel better, and the fears dissipated.

Later, Orlandra and I were blessed to find a two-bedroom apartment. It was October 31, 2005, and I was feeling particularly good because we were scheduled to move into our new apartment. I was headed to work and thinking about how good life had become. As I crossed the street from the bus stop, I was struck by a car. I don't remember much about the impact, but I do remember, as I slipped out of consciousness, hearing a lady say, "Miss, I am praying for you. I am praying for you." I never knew who she was. I do remember waking up in Johns Hopkins Hospital, where I'd been taken by helicopter. I was hurting all over. Both my shoulders were broken. My right arm was broken, my teeth were shattered, and I had no skin on the right side of my face. I was in a bad place. Even as I groaned in pain, I remembered God, who I had come to trust, and I prayed, "Please help me, Father, in the name of Jesus, please help me."

Bad things do happen, even to people who are trying to do good. Since I didn't have insurance, the hospital discharged me after two days. They put a hard cast on my right arm, gave me a prescription for painkillers, and sent me home, even though I was still in pretty bad shape. The pain had really set in. I ached all over. I was bruised and sore. I had to lie flat on my stomach to get relief. The medication the doctors gave me made me feel a familiar high, which I was determined to resist, so I stopped taking it. I took over-the-counter Motrin and worked through the pain. I'd lie on the bed and groan in misery as sharp, penetrating pain tore through my body. As my wounds began to heal, the pain began to lessen, and I learned that faith could do what drugs could not. I knew with God's help that I'd make it—and I did.

My support team from T.A.M.A.R's Children was right there when I got home. They cleaned the house, cooked for me, bathed me, and encouraged me. Since I was in no condition to take care of Orlandra, my resident manager, Michelle, and her mother volunteered to care for her. At first I was very reluctant. However, Michelle promised to bring her to visit me every day. Taking away my baby was a trigger, and I almost fell into that familiar, dark place, but Michelle did what she promised. Every day she brought my beautiful little girl to see me.

Thirteen days after my thirty-eighth birthday, I moved into our new apartment. I was still recovering from the accident. My arm was in a cast, and I had scabs on my face. I looked horrible, but I was excited. Now Orlandra and I both had our own bedrooms. Around this time, Joan Gillece, cofounder of T.A.M.A.R's Children and an expert in trauma, began mentoring me. She allowed me to participate on a team of mental health experts who trained social service workers about trauma. It was an exciting time. I was actually standing in front of audiences as a member of a professional team and explaining what trauma was and the impact it had on women's lives. I called us the "Dream Team." For me it was beyond what I had ever dreamed. I'd come from being a scared little girl who'd been raped and molested to a teenager with a baby and an abusive husband to a coke-snorting, crack-smoking, street-walking prostitute to a member of a respected and sought-after team of mental health professionals. It was more than a dream come true—it was the grace of God! Traveling and spending time with Joan changed my life. She believed in my voice, and she believed my voice needed to be heard.

The first time I stood in a training conference and told my story, I was greeted by a standing ovation. I was overwhelmed. All I'd done was tell the stark-naked truth. I'd not dressed up what had happened to me. I'd told it honestly. There were times in my presentation when I thought I couldn't explain or tell completely what had been done to me. Then I realized how I'd been healed, and how by telling my story someone else like me may be healed. So for the first time in my life, I held my head up and shared in detail what had been done to me. Although T.A.M.A.R's Children had guided me down the road to healing, the journey was not over. Every day was another step toward completion.

I now had Orlandra, a job, and a home. We lived in that two-bedroom apartment for two years until Habitat for Humanity accepted me into their program and agreed to build us a new home. That part of my journey was not easy. Johns Hopkins Hospital had reported me to the credit bureau for nonpayment of services after the hit-and-run accident, and, in 2007, Andi informed me that T.A.M.A.R's Children was closing.

Orlandra and I saw the groundbreaking of our new home. She held a pen and I helped her write her name on a board that went into the framework of the house. I worked every day with the volunteers from Habitat for Humanity, until the last nail was driven on December 28, 2007. They handed me a key, and the same Tonier Johnson Cain who'd lived under the bridge at the overpass moved into a brand-new house. I was a home owner! It was a feeling I couldn't begin to describe.

Orlandra and I lived in that home until October 2011, when we were forced to move because the neighborhood had gotten so bad. Gangs and crime had now taken over the community, and an entire new group of young women had replaced me on the streets. New dealers were selling drugs to abused and traumatized people. One day I came home and discovered that dealers were using my mailbox as a place to hide their drugs. Another time I came home, and they were sitting on my steps. The neighborhood had become unsafe. I knew what these people were capable of doing. I wanted to warn them of what was ahead, but I knew they wouldn't listen, just like I wouldn't have listened ten years ago. I didn't dare expose my daughter or myself to the dangers, so I moved.

In some ways, I felt like I was living out the theme song from *The Jeffersons* sitcom: "Moving on up to the East Side, to a deluxe apartment in the sky." We didn't move to a penthouse apartment; we just moved to a condo in Annapolis. When we moved into that unit, I was reminded of the days when I wouldn't even have been admitted on the grounds of a place like this. I remember looking around that condo and thinking how blessed I was. I couldn't help but remember that, but by the grace of God, I could've died—yet there I stood as a living testimony to the goodness of God. It was so far away from Allen Apartments, yet it was so near. It would always be near. I didn't forget. I remembered, but I knew I was liberated.

In 2008, Joan hired me to work as the team leader for the National Center for Trauma Informed Care for the National Association of State Mental Health Program Directors. My life had truly changed. I was now traveling across the United States speaking to and training mental health professionals about trauma. It all seemed so surreal that the same Tonier Cain who'd been arrested eighty-three times and convicted sixty-six times was working with the same professionals who'd ignored her plight. Now these people were actually listening and being taught that many of their clients were victims. Finally, the system was listening, and they were listening to me from a platform that had been given to me by Joan. There were many times when I couldn't believe they were actually listening to me, but they were. I was greatly humbled. I knew it was not about me; I was just a voice.

As the concept of trauma-informed care spread in mental health environments, there were requests for training tools. In 2008, I was featured in a documentary called *Behind Closed Doors*, sponsored by the Substance Abuse and Mental Health Services Administration (SAMHSA). This documentary told my story and the stories of three other women who had suffered years of childhood abuse and trauma, and how each of us had been revictimized by the system. The documentary was well received by the mental health community and the general public. As a result, I coproduced, along with Laura Cain, who'd become my best friend (and who is no relation), the story of my life in a documentary entitled *Healing Neen*.

CHAPTER 11

The Healing Process, or Why Trauma Therapy Works

For we wrestle not against flesh and blood,
but against principalities, against powers,
against the rulers of the darkness of this world,
against spiritual wickedness in high places.

—Ephesians 6:12 (NAS)

I magine someone did something to you, something so unbelievable it shaped the rest of your life. Imagine the person who did this to you was someone you trusted. And now you can't tell anyone because there is no one to tell. Imagine spending the remainder of your life trying to escape the pain of what had been done to you. When you do find an escape that takes away the pain, it only works for a short period of time, and you are forced to look for other sources. Imagine that the escapes are harmful. This is a good description of trauma, and, even if you have a really good imagination, you can't really begin to understand it unless you've lived with it.

What is trauma? Trauma is a mortal wounding. Its victims actually have a part of them die. For me, it was Tonier who died. She was replaced by a silent version of herself who everyone called Neen. Tonier was smart and inquisitive. She was a loving child with a head of coarse, nappy hair. She loved to sing. She loved her family. She loved her mother. Neen was quiet. She didn't talk much. She kept secrets. Trauma victims learn early on to keep secrets because trauma operates in secrecy.

In some ways, trauma sounds like a sci-fi movie. It has these little mechanisms that cause a victim to remember and to relive the horror of the trauma they've endured. So escaping the original trauma is hard. These triggers often cause an episode of destructive behavior. This is why I'd enter programs, learn all they had to offer, then have an episode triggered by something that reminded me of the trauma, and I'd self-destruct. I repeated this cycle so often that people who knew Neen said that I'd surely die in the streets. I was diagnosed as being bipolar. In jail, the personnel said I was "crazy." I had to be crazy; no one in her right mind would act like did. That is what I thought.

In retrospect, I can understand why counselors, judges, lawyers, and even family members thought I was suffering from a mental disorder. The symptoms exhibited by people who have been traumatized often mimic those found in people with mental disorders. And since mental health counselors and doctors are trained to recognize these behaviors, and because they saw how I behaved, I was misdiagnosed. I remember looking at myself and thinking, *Maybe I am crazy.* My actions were not the way a "normal" person behaved. I mean, who in his or her right mind would live under a bridge? So people looked at my behavior and deduced that I was suffering from a mental disorder. Their solution was to medicate me, but medication didn't address the trauma I'd suffered.

While those early interventions were meant to be helpful, they all failed because they were aimed at treating my outward behavior and not what was hidden deep within that had caused the behavior. It wasn't until I discovered T.A.M.A.R's Children that the root of my trauma was dealt with. Its methods were different from other programs I'd participated in. It focused on what had happened to me, not on my behavior. In the earlier programs, I was accustomed to seeing counselors who asked me questions. I was so familiar with their questions, I had memorized the routine. I knew what they expected, and I was smart enough to say what they wanted to hear. I played the "game." And I "won," but really I lost, until I got to T.A.M.A.R's Children, where a therapist asked me, "What happened to you?"

I was not prepared for that question. It caught me completely by surprise. It wiped out my game plan. It destroyed my defenses. I had all the answers to the standard questions counselors asked. But she wanted to actually know what had happened to me. She recognized that something had been done *to* me. That was a shock. I remember looking at her, open-mouthed, and just staring for a moment. No one had ever asked me that question before. Everyone just assumed I had a defective gene. I had even started to believe that there was something defective in me. But this therapist told me that what had happened to me was not my fault and that I was a victim. In fact, I was not just a victim, but a *wounded* victim.

After the initial shock of being asked this question, I revealed things that no one knew but me and God. It hurt to tell, but I had to. My therapist was patient. She never hurried me, even when I repeated episodes. She knew the emotional and physical pain that reliving my childhood and life brought me. Her language and her tone of voice were always even-keeled, never judgmental. When I reached places where the hurt was still too painful to talk about, she'd comfort me by suggesting we end the session or she'd bring me back to the present until I was able to move on. As I exorcised the demons that had become my life, the therapist was a nonjudgmental, benevolent, guiding professional who assisted me through the process. There were many times I wanted to stop. But stopping was not an option because I was no longer Neen; I was starting to become Tonier again. As painful as it was, I kept inching toward the healing that had started.

My healing began that morning in the Maryland Correctional Institution for Women. My soul was healed as I surrendered my life to Christ. I repented. I acknowledged that Jesus was Lord, and He could save me. I was sincere in my prayers, and God heard me. More important, He healed me. When I got up off that floor, I was no longer a sinner. But my saved soul still lived in an earthly body that had been a prostitute and a drug user for many years. Now I started the process of healing Neen physically and emotionally.

The next step in healing was to acknowledge the injuries that had been done to me. This meant facing not only the events themselves but the people who had done them to me. This wasn't easy. There were times it was physically painful to tell some of the things that had been done to me. I'd grown hard calluses over the sore places to protect myself, but trauma therapy pulled off the scabs to expose the rawness to the healing air of truth. I had to face the reality that some of those awful things had been committed by people I loved who should've protected me. It was a difficult reminder of what I'd lived through, but it was a necessary part of my healing.

The side effects of the trauma in my life were the forms of escape I'd chosen to avoid the pain: alcohol and drugs. Both substances allowed me to numb out. So another part of my therapy was confronting these counterfeit remedies and eliminating them. Uncovering the source of my pain eliminated my need for alcohol and drugs. I also learned that I'd never be able to go back to those so-called friends I used to hang out with, and there were people I loved who I'd have to let go. But avoiding destructive tools and situations were not enough; I needed to find positive tools to help me cope with my triggers.

Because trauma therapy is tailor-made for each individual, anyone and everyone can benefit from it. A trauma therapist departs from traditional treatment where people with similar complaints are treated the same because he or she knows that, while the symptoms may be similar, the treatment must be designed for the type of trauma the individual has suffered. This is why trauma therapy has such a high rate of success.

I needed a tool kit designed just for me, a "fitted-glove" treatment plan and not a one-size-fits-all. Everyone needs to discover what works for them in terms of dealing with triggers. Some people exercise. Others go to self-help groups. Some read the Bible. Whatever it is, once a person identifies positive tools to replace destructive coping strategies, healing can begin. I discovered that I love to read, mostly about history, and I love learning about Jesus and finding positive role models. As long as I live, I will remember what happened to me, but now I have positive coping strategies that have replaced the need for drugs and alcohol. When we can replace the destructive coping tools with positive ones, we can become productive members of society.

I am a trauma survivor! I lived through a hellish childhood that led to a nightmare life. I abused drugs. I abused my body. I abused life. I lied, cheated, and stole. If I could do it, I did it. I didn't care. Actually, I did care, but I'd learned as a defensive tactic to pretend not to care. As a trauma survivor, I learned how to cope with hurt that was so painful and so deep-rooted that it had choked Neen and forced her into a shady under-world of prostitution and drugs.

Trauma therapy is so straightforward; it isn't complicated or rocket science. But this doesn't mean it's easy. I thoroughly believe in trauma therapy because it saved my life. I am a living example of its success. Now I travel across the United States telling victims and mental health practitioners to pursue trauma therapy. In this country all the major fact-finding and fact-gathering organizations report staggering numbers about all forms of abuse. While abuse appears to have reached epidemic proportions, there is still hope. It can be confronted, and, while it will never be fully eradicated this side of heaven, trauma victims have hope for a better life. Always remember: Where there's breath, there's hope!

My Message to Survivors

Eight years ago, I didn't believe anyone could help me. I was told I was hopeless and that I'd die in the streets or spend the rest of my life going in and out of prison. I believed what I was told and didn't try to do anything to help myself. It was easier to drink and use drugs, to just numb out—but I was wrong! Nobody deserves a life of hopelessness. We all deserve a life of joy and peace, a life where we can contribute to the world around us.

We all have a purpose in this life. We *all* have a gift; some have many gifts. We were made in the Almighty God's image. Of all the creatures that roam the earth, God created the human race in his image. How do we get back to what we were truly created for? How do we discover what our purpose is? How do we wake up and move through each day feeling safe? How do we escape the feeling of loneliness, darkness, and worthlessness? I can tell you, it's possible! My path to truth and healing was through trauma treatment and my personal relationship with Jesus. Without hope, we can't find faith, and without faith we *can't* move the mountains of stuff in our lives. For so long I believed that I was nothing, and I thought I'd never be anything. But the whole time, unbeknownst to me, I was not only something, I was a conqueror! I survived because I was supposed to. I was destined to be a survivor and a conqueror. I had a purpose designed for me from the beginning of time.

As I look back on my life, I still cry, and I cry and cry some more. But today my tears are not tears of loss but tears of gratitude, relief, and joy. There are still some things in my life that are very painful, especially concerning my kids. Every day I wake up knowing that I have four kids walking this earth, three of which I wouldn't know if I passed them on the streets, and that's painful. But now I know how to deal with my trauma without using drugs, hurting others, or falling into a pity party. I talk to people, I pray, I talk some more, and pray even more. I know now that there's nothing in my life that I can't handle with my friends' and God's help.

I was told that recovery was dealing with your addiction in a positive way, but I needed more than that. I needed deliverance, and I found that only through my relationship with Jesus. I know that sometimes the last thing you want to hear about is

Jesus, God, or the Bible, and I understand your feelings. I felt the same way. Like a lot of people, I'd ask, "Well, where was God when I needed him?" I asked that question many times. What I found out was that He was always there. Even when I didn't want Him, or when I thought I didn't need Him, He was still there *always*! Every time I went out to prostitute, He was there watching over me and protecting me. Every time I put a dirty needle in my arm or when I had unprotected sex with someone, He was there to protect me from HIV/AIDS. Every time I used drugs while pregnant, He was there to protect my babies. He was always with me, even though I was not with Him. I know it's hard to believe in something or someone you can't see. Someone once told me that if all else fails, why not look up to God? Why not try Him? For me, trying Jesus resulted in me living a clean and sober life, raising my daughter, living in a beautiful home, living in peace, having great friends, working for a top-notch organization, and eventually starting my own company. I could go on and on to tell you what Jesus has done in my life and what He's stilling doing. I am walking in the purpose I was made for, my divine purpose. But it's not about me—it's about you and other conquerors. I encourage you to seek your purpose in life, too.

I want you to live the life you're supposed to live. You no longer have to just exist! No, you're supposed to be at peace, to feel safe, to feel loved, and to have all your heart's desires. We've been through so much in our lives. It's time to *live*! I'm excited about what the Lord is doing. Healing is possible for everyone. We conquered the awful stuff this world dished at us. We lived through it and we came out victorious, and now many of us are helping others with their journey. I want to say congratulations to all of the conquerors, and I thank God for the mercy and grace He has given us *all*.

For those of you who are still struggling with your past hurts, I ask you: Why not try Jesus? Yes, I still have life situations that are difficult. We still live here on Earth, so life situations happen. And sometimes I still hurt from past pain I've suffered, but *Glory to God* because now I know I'm not alone. God promises to be with me through the fire. He promises me that I won't burn. I am the last person to doubt God. How can I doubt Him after all He has done and all He is doing for me? I claim victory, peace, favor, and my inheritance as a child of God. I ask him boldly to bless me abundantly, as His word says. I stand firmly on His word and believe in His promises to me. Boldly ask God to give you all that you need. Just ask, and see what happens. Why not try? You have everything to gain and nothing to lose. I promise you that His word is true, and that He is real. I am living proof! I'm excited to see what the Lord will do in your life!

I will pray for each of you always, and ask God to give you peace, joy, the strength to forgive, and healing—His healing! So be blessed and encouraged. God is able! I love each and every one of you.

My Message to Christians

> But anyone who does not love does
> not know God, for God is love.
>
> 1 John 4:8

I write this message to you because as God's people, we can make a difference in an out-of-control world. I've lived through some horrible times. I could've had a terminal disease but for the grace of God! I should be dead but for the grace of God! I should be in jail but for the grace of God! God was the leveling force in my life. He negated all the bad that should've happened as a natural outcome of the life I was living. When I accepted His love and began walking with

Him, all the terrible things I'd done and that I'd become were washed way. I became a new creature in Him. Today, I am a living testimony to the power and benevolence of a living God.

Like Tamar in the biblical story, I did nothing to merit the shame that was brought upon me. Like Tamar, I had my innocence stolen from me. Here the similarities end. I didn't have an Absalom to avenge my wrong. Instead, I hid what was done to me and suffered in silence. And the demons of silence took control of me. The door to my soul was opened by rape, and then pushed open wider by alcohol and drugs, and the demons of my violation controlled my physical body. I was possessed.

The more I was exposed to alcohol and drugs, the greater the control the demons had. I did everything that a person driven by demons could do. I'm not proud of what I became, but God kept me, even when I didn't realize He was there. When my head was nearly bashed in one night many years ago, I screamed "Jesus!" and I believe that screaming His name saved my life that day. I am a living testimony to the power of His name!

It was when I was at the very end of myself that someone suggested I try God. Like most people who've been down, I thought God didn't like me, and that He wouldn't come see about me. All I really knew was what I'd seen in church people—and I didn't really like what I'd seen. I remember standing in front of the church when I was at my worst. The people would come to church in big cars; they'd be dressed so nicely. The women would have on big hats and sometimes furs. They'd be going to church to worship, but when they saw me there, they'd avoid getting close to me. Even the preacher would avoid us street people. Like those in the biblical story of the Good Samaritan, they'd "pass [us] on the other side." No one from the church ever stopped to help or even offer help. Because they were supposed to represent Jesus, I thought Jesus didn't care about me. I was wrong. I thought He wouldn't hear me pray, and that He wasn't concerned about me or my plight. I was wrong. In a jail cell, I prayed. I didn't know the form or fashion of prayer; I just knew I needed help, and there was no one who could help, so I tried God. I cried out to Him in my darkest hour, and He showed up!

God also allowed me to meet Kathy and Kenneth Kenney, who played an invaluable part in my coming to learn about the love of Jesus. Kathy and Kenneth took the time to pray for me, and I'm so glad they did because I know it was the prayers of these two people who kept me safe while I was in dangerous situations. I believe Ann prayed for me, too. It was because of their prayers and the never-ending love of God that I found my way out of the darkness.

I'd like to remind Christians to pray for children. Often, we pray for our children or grandchildren, but we need to pray for all children. I find myself praying for children I see in stores and supermarkets because I don't know what kind of living situations they are in. Sometimes we take for granted that because a child is living in a two-parent home or in a good neighborhood that the child is safe. This isn't true. Recent statistics prove that abuse takes place in the suburbs as well as in the inner city. Abuse takes place among the wealthy as well as the poor. Abuse takes place in all ethnic groups. We Christians must stand in the gap as the repairer of the breach as we pray for the children. Jesus loves the little children!

The church can and must become a "Bethel" (house of God) for all people, particularly children. Churches can intervene early by establishing programs geared toward children. The damage the enemy wants to inflict to our souls usually begins early in a person's life. For me this was at nine years old. If there is early intervention, it could prevent some of the trauma. When children are taught their value and worth in Christ, they are less likely to become victims. If they know they are God's gift and God loves them, they can be taught to report anyone who violates them. Then they won't suffer in silence, like I did. The message of the Gospel is "God so loved the world that He gave His only begotten Son. . . ." If that message in conjunction with other social principles is taught to children, we may reduce some of the abuse that happens to them. We may be able to better protect them, so they can grow into the potential God has for their lives.

The church can and must become a Bethesda, a house of healing and mercy for all. Sometimes the very place where people should be comfortable going to get assistance isn't that place. There will always be people who take advantage of Christian generosity, but we must be more willing to give. People must know they can come to church and not be condemned or judged. For a lot of people living on the edge of society, church must be welcoming. People who are victims need to feel loved. They need to hear and be shown Jesus's message.

We must continue to show the love of the Lord. We must comfort one another. "Finally, brethren, *whatsoever* things are true, *whatsoever* things are honest, *whatsoever* things are just, *whatsoever* things are pure, *whatsoever* things are lovely, *whatsoever* things are of good report; if there be any virtue, and if there be any praise, think on these things" (Philippians 4:8, KJV).

I wish you the mercy of our Lord Jesus, the soon-coming Messiah. Marantha!

Epilogue

The reunion with my son, Joshua, has not taken place yet, but I remain ever hopeful that we will be reunited because "where there's breath, there's hope."

I am so grateful that God has restored my relationship with my son Brandon. We are developing a wonderful bond, and as a result, I learned I am a grandmother of two. I know God will one day restore my other children as well.

My relationship with my mother has improved a great deal, and just as God has begun good works in me, I believe He's doing the same for my mother. She has changed in some ways and she is not the same as when I was child. I know my mother has been through a lot and she dealt with it just as I did. We found ways to cope to survive, and *survive* we did! Thanks be to God.

Acknowledgments

I want to thank:

My family for understanding that I wrote this book to glorify God, I had to tell it raw to give those who are struggling with similar circumstances HOPE!

Daphnee Cherbuim, for praying with me for a year about this book and every area of my life. Daphnee, you inspired me so much to seek God in all that I do and will ever do!

Andi Karfgin, may you rest in peace, and you are in my heart always.

Dr. Joan Gillece, I cannot thank you enough for mentoring me in the field of Trauma Informed Care and for believing in my story. From the first time we met you gave me hope. Your guidance, not only professionally but personally, has changed my life.

Pat Shea, what a wonderful person you are. I am grateful that you were the first person to whom I entrusted my daughter. Thank you for your friendship and for being there for me and my daughter.

Laura Cain, you probably know me better than anybody. As a filmmaker you're brilliant, as a friend you're amazing. So many times, I would tell you my dreams and you always believe that I will one day accomplish them.

Donna Sweeting, I told you what I wanted to do, and you immediately moved forward to help make it happen. In July of 2013 we met, and one month later, we became business partners, but somewhere back in time God had already predestined our bond and friendship, and for that I am eternally grateful.

Kathy and Kenneth Kenney, you took a convict like me out of jail and brought me into your home, fed me, and provided me shelter; this is what Jesus asks of us. With your selfless actions, you've shown me how a Christian should be. More so because of your love and protection for my daughter, I am able to travel and spread the message of hope. You are very much a part of me and this work I do.

Last, but certainly not least, thank you, Dr. JoeAnn Houston, for being an amazing writer. I enjoyed getting to know you during this process. May God Almighty be glorified!

About the Author

Tonier Johnson Cain was born and grew up in Annapolis, Maryland. Her life is a testament to the failed social systems of America. Yet Tonier, through a program designed to address the trauma she had suffered, was able to move beyond her life of destructive behaviors and become a productive citizen.

Today, she is a nationally and internationally sought-after speaker and an authority on trauma-informed care. Tonier attributes her success to her relationship with God and trauma therapy. She still resides in Annapolis, where she is raising her daughter, Orlandra.

Her message is universal: Where there is breath, there is hope!

Tonier Cain may be contacted at: *toniercain.com* or *Speaker@ Healingneen.com*.